NASHVILLE'S
MOTHER CHURCH
THE HISTORY OF
RYMAN AUDITORIUM

Second Revised Edition

by William U. Eiland

Contributing writers, Second Revised Edition

Craig Havighurst & F. Lynne Bachleda

Nashville's Mother Church
The History of Ryman Auditorium
Second Revised Edition

First edition by William U. Eiland
Additional contributions by
Craig Havighurst and F. Lynne Bachleda

Designed by Michael Robertson

Cover photo by Josh Newman

CONTENTS

© 2012 Hatch Show Print

Introduction

All are welcome. It is a sentiment that has been a constant throughout the history of Ryman Auditorium; from its earliest life as a non-denominational tabernacle, through scores of educational lectures, and decades of world-class music, theater, and dance brought to the stage by longtime manager Lula C. Naff. For countless community gatherings, for the Grand Ole Opry and the millions of country music fans it has attracted, and for classic, contemporary, and cutting-edge acts who have taken the stage since the 1994 reopening, the Ryman has always had a way of being perfectly suited for the moment—whatever that moment may hold.

Unlike most historic venues that remain in operation, the Ryman is not an elegant gilded opera house or an exuberant Art Deco movie palace, and was not created with those who could appreciate "high art" in mind. For its first seventy years, it was a public building, Nashville's largest, built by and operated for the good of the people of Nashville. The building was allowed to serve anyone who could rent it, resulting in a fascinating variety of people and events to its credit, many of which are detailed in this book. But equally diverse, and equally important, are the audiences who have filled the hall and supported the building since Tom Ryman envisioned it in 1885.

The generous and welcoming spirit, which placed Ryman Auditorium at the center of the city's cultural life from the start, remains very much a part of the mission today. Stewardship and a sense of responsibility for the National Historic Landmark are wholeheartedly embraced by staff and management. The overarching goal is to ensure that the Ryman will continue to serve, to intrigue, and to inspire all who visit and all who take the stage for decades to come.

Sally Williams
General Manager
Ryman Auditorium
July 2014

Nashville's riverfront at the end of the nineteenth century was a bustling commercial hub with steamships delivering goods to warehouses along Front Street — today First Avenue.

Tennessee State Library and Archives

I. The Tabernacle

At the end of the nineteenth century, Nashville's uncontested preeminence as a cultural, educational, and commercial center for the post-Reconstruction South was a source of great pride to its citizenry. Rapidly modernizing, the city became one of the most important rail centers in the region, having already established itself as a prominent river port. Adding to the hustle and bustle of steamboat and railroad, the first electric streetcars began service in 1889 over the newly paved streets. Nashville was busily distancing herself from the bitterness of the Civil War and joining the ranks of the industrializing cities of America in the Gay Nineties.

To contemporary observers, Nashville's position was evident. It was the main commercial center and market for the entire region; it was a burgeoning financial center; and its publishing and educational establishments gave it prestige throughout the nation. It was for good reason, then, that Nashvillians took pleasure in calling their city the "Athens of the South."

In 1892, Nashville's population stood at 77,000 people. Only twelve years earlier the U.S. Bureau of the Census had given the population as 43,350. This unprecedented growth in part accounted for the development of what has been called Nashville's "Decisive Decade," the years between 1890 and 1900, precisely those years when the Union Gospel Tabernacle became a forum for religious revival, public discussion, and cultural and educational entertainment.

Although urban expansion and increasing industrialization were noteworthy results of its population explosion, so too were social unrest and severe overcrowding. As the "haves" prospered, the "have nots" became more apparent, and Nashvillians became alarmed at such manifestations of social unrest as rising crime, public drunkenness, and pervasive poverty. Lower Broad Street (later known as "Broadway"), with its saloons, gambling, and prostitution, was an affront to those moralists who were being swept along by the strong current of revivalism engulfing the nation.

Revivalism was one response to the social ills and the loosening of those Victorian inhibitions that had traditionally governed behavior, and with the coming of the professional revivalist to town, Nashville's religious and cultural life would never be the same.

The rise of the modern city provided a fertile environment for the professional evangelist. So much sin in such a compact space attracted not only the sinner but the self-styled saint as well. Dwight L. Moody's evangelistic success showed others just how popular, and how profitable, revivalism could be. When local churches proved unable or unwilling to stem the tide of lawlessness and iniquity, the city evangelist stepped in, and by shrewd self-promotion of his message to an event-starved populace, he was often able to effect changes by the sheer force of a powerful personality. Most important, these revival preachers reached many people who had lost contact for one reason or another with local religious institutions.

Samuel P. Jones

Hargrett Rare Book and Manuscript Library,
University of Georgia, Athens

Samuel Porter Jones

Samuel Porter Jones was just such a man. Enormously influential in the South, his impact on Nashville was immediate. Unprepared for his flamboyance, the city did not quite know how to react when he first came to town in March 1885. Nonetheless, what began as a two-day revival sponsored by and within local churches became a longer-lasting spirit of Christian, primarily Protestant, renewal that had far greater results than the Reverend Jones himself would ever have imagined.

If heredity does in fact have the power to shape us, it is hardly surprising that Sam Jones became the leading evangelist of his day. Although his grandfather, great-grandfather, and four uncles were Methodist ministers, it must have been from his grandmother that he got his zeal and determination. It was said that she read the Bible thirty-seven times, each time on her knees, and demonstrated her faith in the otherwise staid hometown church by clapping loudly, shouting lustily, and walking the aisles whenever she felt the presence of the Holy Spirit. She took care of young Sam when he, as he described himself, was a "black-eyed, mischievous, frolicsome lad...so smart that the teachers were compelled to like [me], so bad that [I] acquired a close and practical intimacy with the rod."

Although he imagined himself cut out for greatness, even as a child, Jones spent five years of his early adulthood battling alcoholism. In 1872, at his father's deathbed, he promised to "meet his father in heaven" as penance of having sent the old soldier "in sorrow to his grave." True to his word, he became an itinerant preacher that same year, and his experiences among the rural folk of his north Georgia circuit accounted for his intensely personal and deliberately homespun style of preaching. His pattern of first raking his audiences over the hot coals of hell and then salving their burning wounds with the promise of sweet redemption gained for him a reputation as a fiery, charismatic speaker. By 1883, his fame had spread to the point that he could devote himself to full-time revivalism, and this he did with a vengeance. Such a man invading a town that prided itself on being a religious center was bound to arouse controversy. His blunt and dramatic preaching style aroused ire and indignation among his more self-satisfied listeners and provoked accusations from the religious establishment and the press that he was vulgar, coarse, and even obscene.

In those March revivals of 1885, Jones castigated Nashvillians for their indifference to sin. He painted the city as top to bottom a den of the worst kind of depravity, with the most visible signs of that immorality being whiskey drinking, card playing, dancing, and clubbing—precisely those diversions his listeners at McKendree Methodist Church were most likely to pursue.

Their social clubs he called "gilded deviltry." Dancing was for simpletons, and Jones begged mothers not to debauch their daughters by sending them to "dancing-schools kept by old hook-nosed Frenchmen." The Reverend Jones told Nashville that he had nothing but pity for the poor man upon whom the devil bestowed a society woman and a poodle dog. Other targets for his contempt were gambling, prostitution, circuses, profanity, billiards, dresses "cut down low," baseball ("the most corrupting thing this side of hell"), bicycle riding, prize fighting, and cigarettes ("an effeminate Yankee convention which softens the brain").

Of all human sins, whiskey drinking was the worst. For recovered alcoholic Jones, as he shouted to his audience in Nashville, "every barroom is a recruiting office for hell!" Whiskey may be a good thing in its place, "but its place was in hell!" How, he asked, could any city that licensed eighty-one wholesale liquor dealers and ninety saloons ever raise itself from its quagmire of degradation?

Lashing out at laxity and selfishness, Jones proclaimed himself as a scourge to the good, but not quite good enough, people of Nashville. Louise Proctor Ryman remembered from her elders what "Sam Jones colorfully said after the congregation had just finished singing 'In the Sweet Bye and Bye.' He stood up to preach and announced that his subject was not on 'The Sweet Bye and Bye,' but rather on 'The Filthy Here and Now.'"

For the next two months Sam Jones, the man, and his message were the talk of Nashville. Although many thought he had delivered a timely and necessary inspiration to Nashville's Christian community, others thought colorful language and pulpit histrionics to be decidedly out of place in their city.

Jones himself added fuel to the fire by calling his critics at Nashville's various newspapers "sap-headed reporters." He sometimes came dangerously close to comparing his enemies to dogs but stopped short, as he put it, because he "wouldn't want to hurt the dog's feelings." It was no wonder that, after his departure later in March 1885, some Nashvillians hoped the Lord would spare them the return of Jones and his acid tongue.

But return he did in May 1885 for a series of revivals that Nashville's *Daily American* reported "brought together the largest congregation ever gathered in the South." True to form, Jones never tempered his remarks. Exhorting the people of Nashville to wash off the "devil's fleas," he accused them of every sin imaginable, including some not previously hurled their way—adultery, hypocrisy, and usury.

In spite of critics, Jones's popularity proved so great that plans immediately got under way to provide him with a permanent meeting place for his revivals. He represented a new force in Nashville, and the city's leaders were anxious to use this new social Christianity's emphasis on good works, rather than on grace, for their own ends. Sam Jones's "git up and git" brand of religion was a revelation for a city long viewed as a citadel of traditional Protestantism. The lasting symbol of this muscular Christianity of organized philanthropy and legal temperance reform is Ryman Auditorium.

Thomas Green Ryman
Tennessee State Library and Archives

Captain Thomas Green Ryman

Twenty-three years after the arrival of the first steamboat on the Cumberland River, Thomas Green Ryman was born in south Nashville on October 12, 1841. At an early age, after he and his family moved to Chattanooga, young Tom learned about the ways of river life from his steamboat captain father, fishing in the Tennessee River. That experience quickly proved valuable. By 1860, the family had returned to Nashville, and with the death of his father shortly thereafter, twenty-three-year-old Tom took on the responsibility of helping to support of his mother, brother, and three sisters.

Ryman's fishing business thrived during the Civil War. He sold his catch to both Union and Confederate forces and thereby saved enough money to purchase his first steamboat. To buy it, he had to go to New Orleans, which was an arduous journey in those days. Having sewn $3,500 into his shirt, he refused to take it off even at night. Ryman would later say that he "like to have smothered to death" along the hot, muggy trails to Louisiana before he could buy the boat.

Ryman's first steamboat had the appropriate name, *Alpha*, and it quickly made enough money to enable him to build his second steamer, the *Eddyville*, in 1869. By 1880, he had two shipping companies operating on the Cumberland and lower Ohio Rivers, and in 1885 he consolidated these into the Ryman Line, with a total fleet of some thirty-five steamers.

Although he had little formal education, Ryman was industrious and shrewd. He had to be both to withstand the sometimes underhanded tactics to which his competitors on the river resorted. Physically strong and well-proportioned, he was a tough man who could easily handle the rough and hard-living dock workers he employed.

By some accounts Ryman was also a soft-hearted man who distributed coal to the needy from his own basement, who paid for the funerals of his employees and saw to it that their families did not suffer, and who even had his gardener go out and rake the snow from a magnolia's leaves lest the tree be too much "offended" at the weight.

At times it is difficult to separate the myth of Captain Ryman from the reality. Some versions of his life hold that he was an "extraordinary reprobate," much given to carousing with his rowdies before his conversion. The literature has long held that Ryman owned a saloon on Broad Street, where roustabouts and passengers jostled each other to buy cheap whiskey at a nickel a glass. The legend persists that he went with some of his unruly cronies to Sam Jones's revival tent for the express purpose of disrupting the meeting with heckling and jeering.

Ryman's great granddaughter Charmaine B. Gossett has disputed this story: "The only rowdy crew he took with him to the meeting were [sic] his wife and six children, ranging from age four to fifteen years."

The lore about Ryman's rowdy ways obviously began during his lifetime, as evidenced by an article that appeared in the *Nashville Banner* the evening after his death. The reporter, after having interviewed several of Ryman's associates, attempted to set the record straight, stating, "There has been an idea prevalent that before his conversion at the meeting by Sam Jones, Capt. Ryman was a drinking man and was in fact a bad character." But his associates insisted that Ryman "had never in his life taken a drink over a bar, and that he had never, to their certain knowledge, been drunk." The article insinuates that the rumors of Ryman's character flaws were inventions of his political enemies.

Regardless of Ryman's intentions, the fact remains that during Sam Jones's tent revival in May 1885, Captain Ryman converted to a Christianity of good works, civic virtue, and gospel evangelism. Many writers have said that he became a changed man after hearing Jones speak of the sanctity of motherhood. Complete versions of Jones's sermons from that May do not exist, but it is safe to assume that he painted vivid pictures of a mother's tribulations when her son turns to drink, because elsewhere he brought tears to the eyes of his congregations when he described the good mother grieving over her son's descent into a drunkard's hell.

Again legend takes over where facts are few. Local historians have said that Ryman immediately rounded up his friends, went to his saloon, gathered the whiskey barrels, and poured their contents into the Cumberland. Remarking that "they say even the fish got tipsy," one Nashvillian gave new expression to the tale that Ryman was so beset by remorse over the whiskey trade on his steamboats that he began telegraphing up and down the rivers to his boat captains that they should break up the bars and dump the liquor and gambling tables overboard. However, it is far more likely that he simply let the contracts for bar services on his boats expire and did not renew them. Daisy Ryman Coggins, Ryman's daughter, confirmed that the liquor on board his boats was not his property but that of the concessionaires who had contracted with the company to run the bars. Regardless, it was a costly decision for Ryman, because he lost both his percentage of the bar profits and those customers who would have preferred more rapid rail transport were it not for the liveliness of his shipboard bars and gaming parlors.

On the night of his conversion, Ryman discussed with Jones the idea of building a "tabernacle for all denominations that would be amply large to accommodate the largest crowd." But the campaign for the Young Men's Christian Association building, which was then in progress (and for which Jones would raise much of the money from his congregations), took precedence, and they decided to postpone their plans.

In the meantime, because he had to delay his more grandiose vision, Ryman built a gospel and temperance hall at 57 Broad Street. As he reported in a letter of March 17, 1886, to Reverend Jones, he built the hall for $3,500 with the assistance of another convert and associate, Captain Alex Kendall. The two captains' temperance hall was "run nonsectarian," seated 250 people, and was open every night for an hour.

Captain Ryman also mounted "scripture boards" on street corners and outfitted a gospel wagon to serve as a sort of mobile mission in the city. Its headquarters was the temperance hall, conveniently located next to Ryman's offices. He then had scriptural passages painted over the doorways on his steamers lest passengers ever forgot that they rode on a vessel devoted to God's glory. Ryman revealed to the Louisville *Courier-Journal* that he "believes in the will of Divine Providence and never insures his boats." Indeed, Sam Jones had no more zealous convert.

Yet Ryman still envisioned a grander, more appropriate building for evangelism than his small temperance hall. In 1887, the year after his Broad Street hall opened, Ryman drew the first pencil sketch for the Tabernacle. He dreamed of a building large enough to seat "multitudes." Ultimately, after first using Nashville's eminent architect W.C. Smith (who went on to design the city's Parthenon), Ryman turned to Hugh C. Thompson as the architect and to J.G. Jones to build the foundation. According to a contemporary newspaper account, Thompson agreed to reduce his rates in order to have the honor of building the Tabernacle. Although some critics of the time characterized the structure as graceless, Thompson eventually won admiration from his contemporaries and from modern builders for raising such a broad roof 100 feet from the ground at its peak.

Before the architectural plans could be realized, however, the new Tabernacle needed a site. Ryman and the trustees of the new corporation quickly set out to find a suitable location. Although it had to be centrally located and convenient to public transportation, it could not have "street cars passing the building to annoy the meeting." Ryman's preference for the Summer Street (now called Fifth Avenue) location finally prevailed over those who were in favor of buying the old Broad Street Amusement Hall. In an 1897 interview, he recalled that "after days of hunting among real estate men, we bought the lot on which the Tabernacle stands."

A Charter of Incorporation for the Union Gospel Tabernacle was filed on February 25, 1889. As expressly stated in its articles, its goals were "strictly religious, non-sectarian, and non-denominational and for the purpose of promoting religion, morality and the elevation of humanity to a higher plane and more usefulness." The trustees wasted no time in beginning construction, setting the foundations in the summer of 1889 and raising the walls to a height of six feet by spring of the following year.

The first revival held within the walls of the building occurred in May 1890, before the building was complete. Ryman and his architect raised a tent over the walls and foundations, but in the face of thousands hungry to hear Sam Jones this was merely a stopgap measure. Both Ryman and Jones knew that the building had to be finished before another series of revivals could take place there.

Finding funds was always a problem, and for Ryman, whose overriding passion had become that building, the construction meant a great deal of personal effort, most of it, as he put it, "on the streets." Before his death, Ryman said of his persistent search for money: "I have prayed to God when most people were asleep. I have worked for this Tabernacle hard for ten years. I have neglected my business and paid out money liberally for it. So much have I done this that many people thought I had plenty of money. This is a mistake; I had my heart in it though." Even when it was substantially complete, the new Tabernacle carried large debts for its construction, debts for which Ryman continued to pay interest until his death. Yet for Ryman the building was worth its heavy cost.

Finally, after two more years of construction, the Tabernacle was completed in 1892. Even today this relic of the late Victorian age, beloved by those who experience its warm intimacy, never fails to impress the visitor. But how grand it must have seemed in the 1890s, with its vast roof and the curving spaces of its interior! The building is imposing in its solidity and its unadorned strength, as if earnestness of purpose had been poured into its every brick. True to the purposes stated in its charter, the Tabernacle served as a center

An early photograph of the Ryman shows the decoration along the roofline and the facade.

Nashville Room, Nashville-Davidson County Public Library

for religious revivalism in late nineteenth-century Nashville. In 1893, the trustees invited the famed Reverend T. DeWitt Talmadge to speak in Nashville at a one-night service. So popular was the event that hundreds were turned away at the door. Soon thereafter, the trustees planned another revival, this time featuring the Reverend B. Fay Mills, a celebrated professional evangelist who quickly gained converts wherever he preached.

Mills required a great deal of preliminary work by the local churches before his appearance, including arranging meetings for men only, for ladies only, and for young people only in the various churches. Nearly all of Nashville's Protestant churches planned to participate in this crusade. Advance organization paid dividends in souls, and, if anything, Mills's revival was more successful in fulfilling the goals of the Tabernacle and in unifying Nashville's Christians than even Jones had been, so much so that one of the local newspapers called it "the greatest awakening" in the city's history.

In 1892, the Theodore Thomas Orchestra gave the first concert in the Ryman.

Tennessee State Library and Archives

Sam Jones, of course, made annual visits to raise money for the Tabernacle, but the religious event of the year 1896 was Dwight L. Moody's two-week revival. Four thousand people had gathered in November the year before just to make preparations, and committees and subcommittees of laymen and clergy spent the intervening three months working out the details.

When the time came, Moody moved the city to a new height of spiritual fervor with his spare, gentle eloquence. He was tireless in speaking two or three times a day and to a variety of congregations throughout the city. Such was his influence and popularity that the *Daily American* grandiosely proclaimed Nashville the center of the nation, a claim the editors would repeat for several years to come.

As if to prove the assertion, Sam Jones, the "Moody of the South," came again to Nashville twice during the next year. His first visit in February was for a revival of the sort he had been preaching in Nashville since 1885, but for his second visit, he arrived with a different purpose. Many groups intended to hold conventions in Nashville that year to coincide with the Tennessee Centennial Exposition. One such group, the United Confederate Veterans, promised to bring the largest convention ever held in Nashville to the Tabernacle if it could provide enough space for their meetings. Jones was called upon to help raise the money to build a gallery, or balcony, to provide that space.

Ryman still had Hugh Thompson's original plans for the gallery, which had never been built because of lack of funds. Mindful of the need to save money, he and his committee accepted a low bid of around $10,000 for the iron and steel gallery support construction, the woodwork, and enough seating for 2,500 people. The Louisville Bridge Company did the iron work, anchoring the gallery on steel columns extending to the basement, and the Indiana Church Furnishing Company won the contract for the benches, with a bid of $2,700. J.H. Yeaman did the woodwork for the gallery, and aside from minor work, he and his fellow contractors finished the addition by the end of May 1897. Because they needed hard cash and not pledges for much of their work, the Tabernacle Circle, a group of ladies dedicated to raising $2,000 for the gallery fund, called on Jones to return to Nashville and lecture for an impromptu benefit. Fittingly, on June 4, 1897, Sam Jones, the man who inspired the construction of Union Gospel Tabernacle twelve years before, was the first to stand on the platform on the main floor of the auditorium and speak to the crowds filling the new gallery. The original vision for the building was complete.

On June 22, 1897, the reunion of Confederate Veterans—"the remnant of an army that is rapidly passing away…gray with age and scarred with noble wounds," in the words of Governor Robert Taylor—brought nearly 100,000 people into Nashville, practically doubling the population of the city for three days. Nashville, proud of its progress and delighted to be hosting the Centennial Exposition, responded with a warm hospitality that had its citizens opening homes and schools to the veterans. The Tabernacle served as the

A 1922 view of the stage and Confederate Gallery during a religious meeting

Hardeman Tabernacle Sermons, Vol. 1

group's headquarters and as the starting point for a stirring parade through the streets of Nashville. After receiving such a warm welcome in Nashville, the United Confederate Veterans voted to donate their $2,500 surplus from the reunion toward the gallery fund. Because of the nostalgia they generated and their contributions to the completion of the Tabernacle, the veterans of 1897 left behind a lasting legacy when the Ryman trustees named the new balcony "The Confederate Gallery."

The completed Tabernacle finally conformed to the intentions of Ryman, Jones, and Thompson. It seated an estimated 4,000 people and had cost approximately $100,000 to build. Except for the absence of a stage, the hall looked substantially as it does today, with its gabled, red brick façade set onto a rusticated stone base. Rather than exhibiting the exuberance of late Victorian architecture, its impressive proportions and sturdy pier buttressing are Gothic in inspiration, as are its details: rows of lancet windows, the arcading of the roof parapets, and the pointed arch that frames a dedicatory plaque on the façade. Additional decoration once relieved the spare austerity one sees today. Originally, the building had crest tiles in the form of a row of stylized flowers—such as that found in England's Exeter Cathedral—along the main roofline and crockets (small ornamental carvings) on the gables. Certainly the greatest achievement of its architect is the broad roof, which encloses such a vast space.

The Tabernacle's directors could not easily ignore the public's participation in its construction. Many of them, Tom Ryman included, eventually realized that the Tabernacle belonged not to its trustees but to the people of Nashville, who were demanding that it be used for a variety of purposes. Ryman never lost his conviction that it should not be used for anything morally repugnant or frivolous, but as early as 1892 public education programming entered the Tabernacle when Professor E. Warren Clark gave an illustrated lecture on Mikado's Court, on May 14, 1892. A chorus from Fisk University, Nashville's esteemed African American college, also appeared at this program, thereby helping early on to establish the Tabernacle as a venue for all Nashvillians. Earlier that month, the Theodore Thomas Orchestra headlined the Tabernacle's first musical concert. Thomas was the well-known founder and conductor of the Chicago Symphony Orchestra, and the trustees unwisely hoped that paid admissions to a concert by his orchestra and chorus would pay the cost of his contract to appear. In fact, additional programs were necessary to pay those expenses until the debt to him was finally canceled. His appearance unfortunately had added nothing to the sadly depleted building fund.

As time passed, and particularly after Ryman's death, the trustees leased the building for almost any program that they found suitable and that required a grander space than other buildings in Nashville could provide. They also realized early on that they would have to depend on nonreligious events to bring in much-needed revenue to service the debt.

For the first twenty years of its existence, the board of directors relied on the lyceums and Chatauquas to provide the entertainment demanded by the public. These groups supplied speakers and musicians to localities that would otherwise not have them. Through the services of these organizations, John

Philip Sousa and his band, North Pole pioneer Commander Robert Peary, orator William Jennings Bryan, and Tennessee Governors (and brothers) Alfred and Robert Taylor appeared in the Tabernacle.

Of course, the community also used the building for a variety of other purposes throughout its history. Meharry Medical College had its commencement activities there for many years, and local high schools used it for their graduation ceremonies. Ward-Belmont College and Vanderbilt University sponsored musical series in the Tabernacle, and for a while it served as home to the Nashville Symphony Orchestra and to the Opera Guild. Policemen's associations, the American Red Cross, the American Society for the Prevention of Cruelty to Animals, and numerous ladies' clubs and churches, among others, used the building for fund-raising programs.

Churches in particular rented the Tabernacle for large gatherings. For example, the General Conference of the Colored Methodist Episcopal Church invited the great educator Booker T. Washington to address its convention in the Tabernacle in 1902. Revivals remained an integral part of the Tabernacle story. N.B. Hardeman, Aimee Semple McPherson, Walt Holcomb, Gipsy Smith, and Norman Vincent Peale all conducted crusades from the building and drew crowds to hear their inspirational oratory.

None was more famous or gifted than preacher Billy Sunday, who led revival meetings in the Tabernacle in the 1920s and 1930s. Once, as prominent Nashville attorney and author Jack Norman, Sr., relates, the Reverend Sunday held a service at which he condemned lower Broadway and the red light district of Nashville as "the devil's backbone." He excoriated the city's fathers for allowing such goings on in a so-called Christian city. On this occasion the crowd included two ladies who happened to be employed in that district and had come to hear the famous Reverend Sunday, probably more out of curiosity than genuine interest in salvation. Their curiosity satisfied, they did not remain to be saved. "They arose and started to walk out," said Norman. "When Sunday saw this, he could not resist the chance to further condemn and shouted to the audience. 'See, there goes two daughters of the devil!' Having nearly reached the exit, one of them turned, waved to Sunday, and shouted back, 'Good-bye, Daddy!'"

Taking their cue from the preachers, politicians also found the Tabernacle an appropriate place for large meetings. In fact, the earliest known controversy about the Tabernacle centered on its use during an election. And, despite its exalted credo, the Tabernacle came perilously close to charges of misuse when, in the fall of 1894, it was used for strictly political purposes: hosting the Tennessee gubernatorial election conventions. Both Republicans and Democrats held speaking engagements and rallies there, but shortly thereafter Nashvillians noted that many of the building's backers were staunch Republicans who supported the party's nominee, H. Clay Evans. The Nashville papers, especially the *Daily American*, lampooned this group as advocates of a third political party, "Tabernacleism," with Ryman and his "gang of pseudo-reformers" supporting the "Tabernacle Ticket." When Ryman carelessly stated that he was sure that the Tabernacle Ticket would win, Joseph W. Dillin, from the pulpit of the Tabernacle itself, called Ryman's "gang" a "rag-tag, bob-tail, whop-it-up-together-and-throw-it-in-a-bag-ticket."

The political furor aroused by "Tabernacleism" humiliated Ryman, and he wrote a letter to the *Daily American* on April 7, 1895, to explain new rules for the use of the Union Gospel Tabernacle. After first saying that it had been abused "like all of God's blessings to mortal men," he went on to call for a banishment of politics from its pulpit. In the short run he succeeded in keeping politics out of the building, but eventually the Tabernacle served as a large and convenient forum for political debate and ceremony. Notable examples were the inauguration of Governor Austin Peay in 1923 and a rousing speech by Alfred E. Smith during the presidential campaign of 1928.

Symbolizing the secondary role that religious activities eventually took in the Tabernacle's history were the deaths of the men who had built it and the change in the name of the building that masked its religious foundations. Tom Ryman himself had absolutely refused to countenance any renaming of the building in his honor, but so popular was the desire to honor this son of Nashville by its citizens that upon his death, they took matters out of the hands of his trustees.

Ryman had been ill for several years but withdrew from his business affairs only shortly before his death in 1904. Confined to a wheelchair by injuries sustained in an accident between his carriage and a transport wagon, Ryman worsened in December, and his health was headline news in Nashville. He died quietly on December 23, and the city mourned his passing.

Sam Jones spoke to the thousands who attended his funeral on December 25 in the Tabernacle. People from all walks of life, wealthy and poor alike, paid solemn respect to the man who, with his unostentatious charity, had done so much for their city. They saw the Tabernacle "both inside and out appropriately draped for the occasion," with black and white streamers as well as numerous American flags. Nashville's religious, business, and cultural leaders occupied the 100 seats on or near the stage along with the river men Ryman had known throughout his life, conspicuous in their grief.

Jones choked back tears with a tribute: "I go into the garden of my heart and pluck the rarest and sweetest flowers that ever blossomed there and lay them on his grave." At the conclusion of the eulogies, Jones suggested quietly that it would be appropriate to name the Tabernacle after the man who loved it so well. The *Daily American* reported the overwhelming response: "...as one person the thousands who heard him were upon their feet." Immediately after the funeral, the steamboat men of Nashville reassembled in the Tabernacle and adopted a resolution calling for a change in the name of the building to Ryman Auditorium.

In its edition the next day, the *Nashville Banner* reminded its readers that five years earlier Dr. Ira Landrith had made the same name suggestion as a way of acknowledging the Captain. At the time, Ryman modestly refused to hear such talk, but now, the *Nashville Banner* opined, there could be no more fitting monument to his memory. For many days following the funeral, various groups in Nashville published resolutions urging the new name. Their actions reflected not only respect for Tom Ryman but also indicated a belief that the Tabernacle belonged to the people of Nashville.

A *Nashville Banner* poll of the trustees found that a majority favored the resolution, but change was long in coming. Perhaps the strength of a reluctant minority or, more likely, legal complexities stymied the will of the public, because the official change did not occur until December 20, 1944, by Amendment to the Charter of Incorporation. But for the people of Nashville, the Union Gospel Tabernacle became Ryman Auditorium when they voted with their feet at the Captain's funeral.

Only two years after Ryman's funeral, the news of Sam Jones's death saddened the city. In a fitting departure, he was stricken while returning from a revival, and he died on October 15, 1906, in the sleeping car of the train taking him home to Cartersville, Georgia. Ryman Auditorium hosted a memorial service for the reverend on October 28. Sam Jones's share in bringing the idea of a vast revival hall for all the people of Nashville to fruition had been in some ways as important as Tom Ryman's. If Tom Ryman was the "Father of the Tabernacle," surely Sam Jones was its godfather.

An advertisement for the Nashville debut of New York's Metropolitan Opera

Nashville Room, Nashville-Davidson County Public Library

II. Opera House and Theatre

Even before the deaths of the two men responsible for building Ryman Auditorium, the maintenance and operation of the building had been delegated to a group of civic-minded businessmen. In keeping with the expanded purposes established for the building, the State of Tennessee had granted a group of fifty representatives a new charter for the Union Gospel Tabernacle on May 11, 1901. This document expressed essentially the same goals as the earlier articles, but it charged the trustees with the task of maintaining the Auditorium in good condition for public purpose. The new committee, whose president for its first three years was Tom Ryman, secured pledges of $9,000 toward the remaining $16,000 debt, on the condition that the balance of $7,000 would be raised. Members of the newly formed corporation pledged additional funds during their first meeting, leaving only $3,763 left to raise in order to retire the debt, if all went according to plan.

To this end, Major E.B. Stahlman, owner-founder of the *Nashville Banner*, advised his fellow directors to cooperate with the Philharmonic Society of Nashville in its invitation to the Metropolitan Opera Company of New York to perform in the city. When the ladies of the Society realized that they could not guarantee even half of the $10,000 demanded by the opera company, the directors of the Auditorium decided to go it alone financially. To ensure that the building's meager resources would not suffer, each of the "fifty representative citizens" guaranteed $200 of the Metropolitan's expenses.

However, in order for the Metropolitan Opera to perform in Nashville, Ryman Auditorium would require a proper stage. This problem, which out of necessity had to be solved quickly, would add considerably to the expense of bringing the company to Nashville. Nevertheless, the committee decided that the cost of $750, not to mention the loss of nearly 200 seats, was worth the potential benefit.

During the summer of 1901, a building committee oversaw construction of the new stage while Nashville prepared for the only two performances by the Metropolitan Opera ever given in the city. The organizers spent heavily on advertisements and persuaded the railroads to offer special rates for the occasion. At $5 for the most expensive box seats and $1.50 for standing room, tickets for the opera were steep in a time when the average wage was 22 cents per hour.

Maurice Grau directed the 250-person company of the Metropolitan Opera during its national tour in 1901 with *Carmen, The Barber of Seville,* and *Faust.* The famed principals, Mmes. Calvé, Sembrich, and Eames, traveled apart from the regulars and went only to those cities where they would be performing. Slated for Nashville were *Carmen* on October 23 and *The Barber of Seville* the following night. Ironically, the Union Gospel Tabernacle, the site of Nashville's holy reawakening, played host on its new stage to one of the most infamous women of easy virtue in literature, the feisty Carmen, but art conquers all. The trustees took careful note of her ability to elevate mankind, and even the newspapers glossed over the more unseemly conduct of this most amorous of heroines. Emma Calvé, the soprano who had created the role of Santuzza in *Cavalleria Rusticana* at its premiere, and one of the greatest singers in operatic history, was scheduled but failed to perform as Bizet's naughty wench. For *The Barber of Seville,* the great Polish bel canto soprano Marcella Sembrich, whom Nashville audiences had already seen and admired with the Boston Festival Orchestra, was cast as Rosina.

In spite of the brouhaha over Emma Calvé's refusal to appear, the occasion was a gala one, with the auditorium divided into boxes for the wealthier patrons. The *Daily American's* critic, Ada Scott Rice, praised the thoughtfulness of the audience by noting that the women of Nashville deserved "canonization for the very general leaving of their hats at home." Yet fashion was served. Rice noted with satisfaction that "it was truly a metropolitan audience in the matter of elaborate dress. Appropriate evening dress was much more generally observed *than even at the recent horse show* [author's italics]."

The whole production won extravagant kudos from the Nashville press, and although the debt was not fully erased by the proceeds of the productions, these two performances changed the cultural history of the city. Equipped with a stage large enough to present grand opera, Ryman Auditorium would continue to attract spectacular entertainment to Nashville.

If Sam Jones, who was on a revival tour, remained calm while a harlot, albeit a make-believe one, commanded his stage, legend has it that Tom Ryman railed enough for both of them. He supposedly installed himself at a lectern beneath the stage and fulminated against the ungodly spectacle going on above his head. He is said to have remained there throughout the four acts and preached without drawing breath. Although doubtful, the story underscores a tension between secular and religious aims that persist to this day in American culture. Disputes over the proper uses of the Auditorium would continue.

The Metropolitan's visit to the Tabernacle was a harbinger of a half-century of glamour. All the great stars of opera's golden age eventually played there. The event that foretold its future as a renowned concert hall was the performance in 1904 by one of the greatest and most famous singers of the nineteenth century in America: Adelina Patti, a woman whose singing was synonymous with vocal perfection.

Madame Patti first sang in Nashville in 1859, and by 1904 she had passed into opera legend. For twenty-three years she reigned supreme in Covent Garden, undeniably the idol at whose feet England's opera-loving audiences worshiped. In Nashville, she sang not only the great arias for which she was celebrated, but also a selection of the sentimental tunes that were popular at the time, including her famously moving rendition of "Home, Sweet Home." Unfortunately for Nashvillians, a janitor chose a moment midway through this song to shovel coal into the two big stoves at the front of the auditorium. The interruption disconcerted Madame Patti for only a moment; she overcame the noise by singing much louder.

The appearance of the greatest of singers was a herald for the great opera stars who came to the Ryman after Madame Patti. For the quantity and quality of musical events on its stage, the Ryman's history as a showcase of the great artists of opera's golden age is unrivaled in the history of the United States. Other cities may have had more elaborate productions, but no other city boasted such a varied, rich schedule.

In its first twenty years, the Ryman hosted an international who's who of musical artistry: the Australian coloratura soprano Nellie Melba, the Italian baritone Giuseppe Campanari, the French diva Emma Calvé, the impresario-singer Bessie Abbot and her company, and Czechoslovakian violinist Jan Kubelik.

In fact, Ryman Auditorium became a favorite stop for celebrated violinists in the early part of the century: Russian Jascha Haifetz and Ukrainian Mischa Elman both came to the Ryman many times in their careers, whereas Austrian Fritz Kreisler and America's own Yehudi Menuhin both openly admitted their admiration for the building's near-perfect acoustics, providing a possible explanation for its popularity among violin virtuosos.

During these decades, a cavalcade of great singers came and conquered Nashville: Emma Eames, Louise Homer, Ernestine Schumann-Heink, David Bispham, Mary Garden, Alessandro Bonci, and Luisa Tetrazzini. Marian Anderson performed in her turn, as did Lily Pons, Alma Gluck, Giovanni Martinelli, and John McCormack. Tom Ryman's own son, Paul, a tenor, sang at the Ryman in 1917 as did Woodrow Wilson's daughter, Margaret. Two of the biggest names in opera appeared back to back in 1919. That week, with performances by both Amelita Galli-Curci, who played the Ryman several times, and Enrico Caruso, who only played it once, is often cited as the most glorious in Nashville's long musical tradition.

In 1908, the virtuoso pianist and celebrated composer Ignace Jan Paderewski made the first of many visits to the stage. From the beginning, he lived up to his billing as the greatest instrumentalist since Paganini, but he, like others before and after him, took exception to the rudeness of his audience. He walked off the stage, midnote as it were, when the noise of departing patrons distracted him during an encore. Chastened, those in a hurry to go to their carriages stood stock-still when the general applause coaxed him to return to the piano.

The touring opera companies came: the San Carlo in the 1920s and Charles F. Wagner's in the 1930s and 1940s. Great conductors brought their orchestras: Walter Damrosch and the New York Symphony Orchestra, Modest Altschuler and the Russian Symphony Orchestra, Eugene Ormandy and the Philadelphia Symphony Orchestra, and Victor Herbert and his orchestra. Bandleaders came: Giuseppe Creatore, John Philip Sousa, Paul Whiteman, Wayne King, Spike Jones, and Fred Waring.

Dancers introduced Nashville audiences to the new American ballet. Isadora Duncan demonstrated "free form"; Ruth St. Denis shocked with her scanty costumes; Anna Pavlova, the "Polish Swan," interpreted the classics; Ted Shawn and His Men Dancers set many a heart aflutter with their athletic interpretations; and Vaslav Nijinsky danced for a very small audience under the watchful, jealous eye of ballet impresario Serge Diaghilev, who stood in the wings. The touring companies brought the classics of ballet to Nashville: the Jooss Ballet with *Coppélia*, Sadler Wells with *Les Sylphides*, the Ballet Russe of Monte Carlo with *Prince Igor*, and the American Ballet Theatre with *Swan Lake*.

By 1908, musicians and singers were not the only performers to enjoy the famed acoustics of Ryman Auditorium. Nashville audiences had heard several distinguished speakers there. Besides evangelists, such notables as Carry Nation and Frances Willard had spoken out against strong drink. Lectures such as Lorado Taft's on sculpture and Elbert Hubbard's on "The Work of the Roycrofters" had instructed Nashvillians in the fine arts. Local professors had taught everything from ethics and humor to crafts and engineering from the stage.

None of the speakers of the time, however, could have enjoyed the same reception as Nashville's most famous visitor of 1907. On October 21, the city donned its "gala attire" for the arrival of President Theodore Roosevelt the next day. The *Daily American* reported that the President was on his way in his special train, *Magnate*, and that "on the arrival of the Presidential [car] a salute of twenty-one guns will be fired from Capitol Hill in the President's honor. The salute will be a signal for the bells and whistles of the city to take up the work of announcing to the people of Nashville that the President has arrived." Advising further that the city had arrayed itself "in the gayest dress, perhaps of its entire history," the newspaper predicted that the crowds would "fill every available inch of the roped-in sidewalks, crowd every window on the line of march and pack every point of vantage from which the distinguished visitor may be seen."

The city had decked itself in bunting, rope, flags, and "teddy bears enough to stock a zoo." Paintings of scenes from the old Rough Rider's life decorated the various intersections that he would pass. The last one, depicting him as President, hung from the roof of the Ryman. The newspapers urged those Nashvillians "on tiptoe with excitement" to get to the Auditorium early because it was sure to be jam-packed for Roosevelt's address.

And it was. The President, buoyed by the contagious cheering he heard on the way to the Auditorium, stood up in his carriage the whole way and "was as full of enthusiasm as a college boy." The building was ablaze with color and noisy with welcome. The planners had taken great pains to segregate all Vanderbilt University students because of their reputation for raucous and boisterous behavior. They proved the organizers correct when the President expressed his admiration for their football team. So often was he interrupted by spontaneous salvos of "Bully" from the adoring crowd, he spoke longer than anticipated. Declaring himself delighted with his reception in Nashville, he spoke on the purposes of his trip, a study of the problems of the Mississippi Valley region and how best to implement reform and bring about economic prosperity.

After leaving the Auditorium, his entourage visited Vanderbilt and Peabody College, where the overjoyed students greeted him merrily with a special cheer:

"Rah, rah, rah, rah, rah, rah
Teddy Bear, Teddy Bear
Boo oo-oo-oo"

While at Andrew Jackson's home, the Hermitage, he charmed his hosts by the courtesy with which he accepted welcome from the former President's granddaughter, Mrs. Rachel Jackson Lawrence. She gave him a tour of the mansion and presented him with a hand-carved hickory stick. The gift must have been the occasion for his reported remark: "By George, this is the kind of stuff I like when I hunt bears." In farewell to the city, he vowed to return; with a final "so long," he left on his presidential train car, Magnet, to conquer other cities with his infectious good nature. The Ryman had served the city well on an historic occasion when its citizens cooperated in a rare display of public spiritedness and municipal pride.

Other noted speakers followed President Roosevelt to the Ryman: socialist Eugene V. Debs; suffragette Sylvia Pankhurst; founder of the Boy Scouts Sir Robert Baden-Powell; civil rights activist and educator Booker T. Washington; advocate for the blind Helen Keller, with her teacher Ann Sullivan Macy; First Lady Eleanor Roosevelt for the Girl Scouts; and famed aviator Eddie Rickenbacker.

Two of the great humorists of the twentieth century spoke in the Ryman. The beloved Will Rogers charmed the city with his appearances, and W.C. Fields must have mightily disturbed Captain Ryman's ghost when he proclaimed on stage that the best cure for a hangover was the application to the throat and stomach of the juice of three bottles of whiskey.

Some who came to speak on behalf of various causes were better known as actors than as orators. Rudolph Valentino spoke out against the way the Hollywood studios manipulated his fellow actors. Francis X. Bushman and Beverly Bayne lent their support to the Nashville Red Cross's war work, and Charlie Chaplin appeared in order to sell Liberty Bonds for the allied cause in World War I.

Ryman Auditorium's glittering roster of performers gave luster to Nashville's past as "The Athens of the South" and prepared the city for its future as "Music City USA." Early in its existence, Ryman was established as and considered a first-rate venue to anyone—politician, orator, preacher, singer, pianist—who could judge the high quality of its sound. These and others found in that wooden, circular interior a perfect environment: where a whisper had the resonance of a shout, where a pianissimo sounded as clear as a fortissimo—in short, a superior theatre.

Although Nashville had seen two grand opera performances in the Auditorium, they had not yet seen a "grand" theatrical event. When news made the rounds that Sarah Bernhardt planned an appearance on March 8, 1906, theatre lovers in the city considered it the cultural event of the young century for Nashville. To accommodate the production and to avoid the problems of the past, the board authorized Mr. J. Gordon Edwards to improve the stage by extending and squaring it off at front, thereby removing two sections of seats. The alteration was to include the addition of dressing rooms and storage cabinets, but Mr. Edwards apparently never got around to finishing them. From an early photograph of a rehearsal in the Ryman, we know that the management used curtains to hide the dressing space and that the chorines actually put on their makeup in pews.

Arriving on a special railroad car designed just for her use, Sarah Bernhardt brought her entire Parisian company to Nashville. Before the end of her long, glorious career, she had toured the United States nine times, but the tour that brought her to Nashville in 1906 was the most unusual and billed as her last, one of many "farewell tours." She refused to accept the dictates of the Theatrical Syndicate, which held a monopoly on theatre bookings at the time. Instead, she took her troupe to tents, schoolhouses, and other nontraditional playhouses. Her disagreement with the guild explains her appearance in the Ryman; normally she would have been booked into the elegant Vendome Theatre a few blocks away.

Pews, a naked light bulb, basins, and curtains marked the spot in the corner of Ryman Auditorium where chorines (chorus girls) and dancers applied makeup.

Special Collections, Vanderbilt University Library

Although sixty-one years old at the time, Bernhardt nonetheless recreated her most famous role: the young, consumptive courtesan, Camille. According to the *Nashville Banner*, no more brilliant or larger audience, 3,140 people, had ever witnessed a dramatic event in Nashville. "The Divine Sarah," no longer young and never so beautiful as Dumas's tragic heroine, captivated the audience and held it spellbound with her embodiment of the pitiful, doomed lady of pleasure. Although speaking French, she used the "golden bell" of her voice and her magical talent for expressing physical agony to enthrall her audience with the sad tale of love lost, love regained, and lost again. Tears of sympathy flowed when Mlle. Gautier died in Armand's arms. Bravas soon followed.

Such a theatrical event was not yet standard fare at the Ryman and would not become so until the 1930s, when the venue's longest-tenured manager Lula C. Naff began to make the Auditorium "the most talked-about one-night stand on the road."

Lula C. Naff, "high priestess" of the Ryman
Francis Robinson Papers, Vanderbilt University Library

Lula C. Naff

Until her retirement in 1955, Lula C. Naff, who preferred the more businesslike "L.C. Naff," was the acknowledged "high priestess of the Tabernacle." Naff had been convinced of the Ryman's potential as an entertainment venue while attending Adelina Patti's concert back in 1904. Her love affair with the Ryman, an attachment she herself dated from that night when Patti's voice resonated so splendidly in the hall, would later make it one of the most famous houses for music and theatre in the business. She never considered her "child," the Ryman, as a relic of a bygone era. Rather, she saw it as a vital showplace whose churchlike interior deserved to be filled to overflowing with "congregations" worshiping at its dual altar of music and theatre. In time, she and the building she loved so well became the grand old ladies of Nashville's community of the arts, but her work did not stop at the borders of the city or even at those of the state of Tennessee. Naff and the Ryman matured and grew famous together; both were hot topics of conversation among "show folk" who visited.

When it was suggested to her that she worked too hard in promoting the building, Naff tartly responded that her labor kept her too busy to succumb to the high blood pressure and heart trouble that seemed to plague her less well-occupied friends. When age finally forced her to retire, Naff complained that she was resting too much: "If they'd just give me the Ryman back, with its dust and paint and a big block of tickets, I wouldn't ask anything else," she wrote to her friend Francis Robinson. The building was her life, as she put it, and indeed it never had a more vigorous defender or a more vociferous advocate. Whether from journalists, city councilmen, artists, or her own trustees, she allowed no criticism of the Ryman to go unanswered, no slight to go unnoticed.

Born in 1875, Naff, a young widow and single mother, moved to Nashville with the Delong Rice Lyceum Bureau as its secretary and bookkeeper in 1903. She was the booking agent for the Ryman in effect long before she had the job in fact, because the Rice Agency provided the course of popular entertainment for the building until 1914. In that year, the indomitable Naff, rather than find other work when the Bureau dissolved, leased the building on her own. For the next four years, she rented the Ryman on an annual basis and by 1920 had shown herself so capable that the governing board reorganized around her.

Naff realized from the beginning that the traditional lyceum mixture of moralizing lecturers and "light" entertainers was unable to draw sufficiently large audiences to make her venture worthwhile. As she put it, "Who wanted to hear Billy Sunday when they could go see Mary Pickford for a dime?" If a "star entertainer" was touring, she endeavored to attract him or her to the Ryman. In such fashion she was able to bring to Nashville, in addition to those stars already mentioned, dramatic sopranos Rosa Ponselle, whose two trips were widely publicized; Geraldine Farrar, who had her own contingent of groupies, the Nashville Gerryflappers; and actors Walter Hampden and Fritz Lieber, who brought Shakespeare's plays to the stage. She also cooperated with various Nashville groups to bring in such musicians and singers as Artur Rubinstein, Frieda Hempel, Maria Jeritza, Marion Talley, and Beniamino Gigli.

Numerous stories about the sharp-tongued manager of the Ryman eventually circulated throughout the nation, but none gained more currency than her earliest "coup." Undaunted by the wariness of her advisors and firm in her resolve to bring the very best entertainers to the Auditorium, Naff contracted with the opera singer John McCormack for his only southern appearance of the year 1916. His management demanded a guaranteed fee of $3,000, an amount most people would have considered prohibitively high for a city the size of Nashville.

A view of the Ryman interior shows the Confederate Gallery curving around to the back wall behind the stage.

Special Collections, Vanderbilt University Library

To publicize the concert, Naff did not deny the widely circulated rumor that she had taken a second mortgage on her house to underwrite McCormack's performance, and she continued to repeat the story countless times in her later years. Knowing its value as publicity, Naff gave the story new life when she again used it to announce McCormack's last appearance in the Ryman in the 1930s: "There is no mortgage on the home, but again John McCormack, World's Greatest Lyric Tenor, will sing at Ryman Auditorium, Nashville, Monday evening, October 12, [1936]." The strategy worked, and the singer sold out the house one last time.

In spite of her brusqueness, Naff was masterful in manipulating the media for the purpose of advertising events at the Ryman. She certainly was not above a little selective arrangement of the facts when she believed that the newspapers were ignoring her schedule. Many letters of congratulation from agents prove the contention that she was an "A-1 publicist." In the specific case of John McCormack's concert, she actually had only the original mortgage on her house at the time of the booking. In a letter in Francis Robinson's papers at Vanderbilt University, Little Rust, her friend and attorney, revealed, "The McCormack concert of 1916 is history. Even though the story that she put a mortgage on her house is a good one, no mortgage was ever signed, and $3,000 was cleared on his performance." Although there was in fact no second mortgage, it is safe to say that Naff was willing to bank everything on McCormack's appearance—and with good cause.

McCormack was a concert favorite throughout the nation. The great Irish tenor had sung with major companies in Europe and the United States and in 1916 was between three-year stints with the Metropolitan Opera. Enrico Caruso was better known but hardly more beloved than John McCormack. The sublime artistry of his phrasing, the exquisite purity of his voice, and the intuitive feeling of his characterizations made him an operatic legend, but it was for the ballads and folk songs of his native land that he was most revered. He was a genuinely popular man whose radio broadcasts were avidly followed by his thousands of fans. Certainly, his fame and appeal foretold success for Naff's brash venture.

At first she may have had real cause for alarm. She worried about the lack of interest in the concert, but she sprang to action. As would remain her habit, she carried around handwritten publicity releases; she also frantically put up posters, passed out handbills, and hawked her show on the streets.

In fact, she succeeded so well that three days before the tickets were to go on sale to the public, she found that she had none left, having already sold all the available seats by mail or through reservations. When she finally opened her office for the public sale, she found a block-long line of people waiting, and rather than refuse them places she sold standing-room-only seats, and, for a slightly higher price, seats on the stage itself.

When she finished, Naff found that she had sold more than 5,000 tickets for a building that normally strained to admit

4,000. She later joked that some people had more confidence in her abilities to sell out the concert than she did, because scalpers sold tickets at the door for $25 each, many times the face value of the tickets. Naff placed patrons in every available square inch of space. More than 300 ended up on the stage with John McCormack, for whom a narrow alley was left so that he could walk to the grand piano. The good-natured tenor turned his back on the thousands before him for one song so that he could sing directly to the hundreds forced to sit behind him.

After the concert, Naff slyly maintained that she had made enough money to pay off both mortgages on her house with enough money left to venture on other artists. No wonder that of all the many artists she introduced to Nashville, McCormack remained her favorite. In fact, she dated the real beginning of her career from his concert in 1916. She herself gave the best review of his performance: "But oh! It was wonderful…when he'd sing, it was the sweetest thing you ever heard—made you romantic enough to fall for it." This was high praise indeed from a woman known for her abruptness and no-nonsense approach to sentimentality.

After this triumph, Naff went on to many others, but the concerts by McCormack, Galli-Curci, and Caruso made Nashville aware of a new spirit at the Ryman. The board also realized that finally they had found the right manager for a building still carrying a debt of some $6,000. It was badly in need of repairs as well as additional funds to sustain the world-class entertainment that Naff had shown herself capable of booking. According to *The Tennessean*, prominent Nashvillian Bernard Fensterwald originated a plan whereby a new group of directors would lease the Auditorium for fifty years. This group formed an operating company, the Auditorium Improvement Company, "to underwrite the present mortgage of about $6,000, provide improvements to the building, including adequate heating and lighting systems, decorations, improved sanitation, and other means to render the building safe and…to assume the costs of ordinary repairs and insurance."

The new board, composed of some of Nashville's most distinguished business and professional men, agreed to contribute $15,000 to pay off the mortgage and pay for the noted improvements. They in turn were to be repaid from the Ryman's gate receipts. Wisely, they hired Naff as the manager of the Ryman. She proved in short order that their faith was not misplaced: she paid off the $15,000 note within the next three years and never operated a single year with a loss.

The new charter, issued September 20, 1920, declared that the Auditorium Improvement Company was "operated without profit to any individual, for the improvement of this building and for the better education and amusement of the people of Nashville." Although the references to moral elevation and religious functions were gone, the charter remained essentially faithful to the ideals of social philanthropy popularized in the city by Sam Jones.

Thus the Naff decades saw great changes in the Ryman's schedule and in the very building itself. Most importantly, the Auditorium became a legendary one-night stand for some of the greatest names in American stage history.

In those golden years of theatre before radio and movies, the "road" had been a lucrative source of revenue for troupes large and small, famous and unknown, good and bad. In those days Nashville had been a "dog town," one in which plays were tried out "on the dog" before they moved to the supposedly more sophisticated New York City. The Ryman's astute manager looked around in 1931 and noted that her building was the only one large enough to offer legitimate theatre; all the others had been virtually eliminated or converted into movie houses.

Other commentators had already declared the "road" a dead-end, the "dog" without any bite, and legitimate theatre itself a cadaver. Some even questioned why first-rate dramatic productions needed to go into the boondocks in the first place, and once there only to suffer poor houses and cultural ignorance, believing it better to give the provinces a steady diet of Shakespeare's proven standards and an occasional vaudeville revue. Most of these same people generally placed the blame for the sad state of affairs squarely at the doorstep of the motion picture studios. Films had robbed the legitimate stage of its

Show bills tout appearances by stage divas Ethel Barrymore and Tallulah Bankhead.

Nashville Room, Nashville-Davidson County Public Library

vitality, they argued, and it would better serve those loyal followers in the large urban centers if it stayed away from the hinterlands' fickle, ignorant public.

Naff proved all these doomsayers dead wrong. Dismissing such arguments as uninformed, she made Nashville one of the earliest and most profitable stops on the slowly reviving "road," even during the worst times of the Great Depression and World War II.

Naff had three criteria for the shows she sought to book. First of all, she knew that she could overcome the waning public enthusiasm for theatre by bringing in big stars. Over the next thirty years, she brought in Irene Castle, Gertrude Lawrence, Katharine Cornell, Maurice Evans, Alfred Lunt and Lynn Fontanne, Bela Lugosi, Clifton Webb, Judith Anderson, Walter Huston, Eva Le Gallienne, Everett Marshall, Joe E. Brown, Melvyn Douglas, Harpo Marx, and Mae West. At the time of their Ryman debuts, some actors had yet to make "big-name" status. Among these included Doris Day, Tyrone Power,

ZaSu Pitts, Orson Welles, Ann Blyth, Basil Rathbone, and Ethel Waters, and others.

Second, Naff believed that she could sell out the house without a "name" in the cast if the play itself was of recognized quality to assure general interest. Thus she presented *Strange Interlude*, *Mister Roberts*, *The Student Prince*, and *Oklahoma*. One of these, *Tobacco Road*, which came twice to Nashville, caused Naff to go to court to prevent the municipal authorities from censoring it for its coarse portrayal of extreme poverty in the rural South.

Third, and the best possible alternative, was the "big play" with the "big stars." Such vehicles were a mainstay of Naff's seasons and included Tallulah Bankhead in *Reflected Glory* and *The Little Foxes*; Helen Hayes in *Mary of Scotland* and *Victoria Regina*; Paul Lukas in *Watch Along the Rhine*; Colleen Moore in *Cindy*; Eddie Bracken and Gary Merrill in *Brother Rat*; and Ethel Barrymore in *Whiteoaks* and *The Love Duel*. Possibly the best example was Naff's presentation of *The Philadelphia Story* in 1941, a performance Minnie Pearl thought the most memorable of the non-Opry events in the Ryman's history. The cast included Katharine Hepburn, Van Heflin, and Joseph Cotten, who played before a standing-room-only house.

Naff, of course, did not have a full schedule of theatre every year. In fact, some years, the theatre offered slim pickings for the fastidious Naff. She filled in her schedule with appearances by such diverse artists as Lily Pons, Alicia Alonso, Lauritz Melchior, Patrice Munsel, Dorothy Lamour, Victor Borge, and the Ink Spots, the earliest documented African American pop group to perform at the Ryman. Martha Graham and José Greco brought their dance companies. Gene Autry may have had bigger box office receipts, but Roy Rogers delighted Nashville's children by bringing along wife Dale Evans and his famous horse Trigger. The Ted Mack Amateur Hour held its program in the Ryman in 1952. Peruvian soprano, Yma Sumac, whose vocal range was said to be well over four octaves, tested the acoustics and raised the roof with her high-pitched warbling. The famous and not-so-famous jockeyed for position on the Ryman's busy schedule.

The Ryman, however, was known nationally as a must-stop on the road for theatrical companies, especially after Brock Pemberton, famous for his writings on the state of contemporary theatre, gave it national attention in an article of 1939. He called it "one of the most unusual" showplaces in the nation, and he named Naff "the most picturesque manageress" in the business. Katharine Cornell and Alexander Woollcott also spread the fame of the Ryman with humorous anecdotes about the idiosyncratic Naff and her Tabernacle-turned-playhouse.

Of course, the old Tabernacle had not been originally designed for major stage productions, and it had changed little since the stage was enlarged to give Sarah Bernhardt room enough to expire in consumptive spasms. Others were afraid that the dusty, unsanitary backstage area might cause them a similar, unapplauded, actual end. The accommodations were primitive and rudimentary, and even the stage itself was insufficient for such large-scale spectacles as *Mary of Scotland*.

Although opera divas may have been content to put on their makeup in screened pews, and Valentino himself may not have complained about dressing in a curtained-off corner, actors were not so eager to suffer such hardships for the sake of a one-night stand. Ethel Barrymore brought her own portable dressing room, a canvas cubicle no bigger than a phone booth. When the story spread that Barrymore retreated to her little dressing room to engage in secret her habit of tippling between Acts I and II, Naff had to scotch the rumor.

The great actress Maude Adams was not as hardy as Barrymore. She might have had to fly around dusty rafters as Peter Pan earlier in her career—and had done so at least twice in Nashville—but now that she was older and justifiably celebrated as a theatrical institution, she accepted no unnecessary discomfort. Just as Naff was ready to sign the contract for the appearance of Adams and Otis Skinner in their revival of *The Merchant of Venice* in 1932, she received a telegram from the star's manager informing her that because she had just learned that there was no running water in the dressing room backstage, Miss Adams would not appear. Little did Adams know that were it not for her hasty cable she would not even have had a dressing room. Naff had a space built according to her specifications: a small room that, ironically, later became the exclusive property of the male stars of the Grand Ole Opry. But for a little while, women had a serviceable dressing room, thanks to Maude Adams.

Helen Morgan, the torch singer who came to the Ryman in 1936, found Adam's legacy to her fellow troupers, the dressing room, unbearably cold. Maintaining that she could hardly sing through chattering teeth, she dispatched her unlucky manager to find a portable heater, even though all the stores downtown had already closed for the day. He finally found one in the nick of time, and a warmed Morgan sang her sultry tunes.

Fanny Brice appeared in Billy Rose's *Crazy Quilt* before Maude Adams had raised the ruckus over the dressing room. The famous comedienne may have suffered inconvenience, but she certainly had her priorities straight. Even on the day of her performance, she remained unaware that female members of shows had to dress in a small, cramped bathroom off the lobby, truly a "water closet" in every sense of the phrase. Brice's manager delayed telling her until the last minute. Finally, after working up his nerve, he approached the lady and began, "Miss Brice, I want to tell you that you have to dress in…"

"Never mind where I have to dress. How is the house?" she snapped.

Hoping to dodge the bullet, the gentleman happily replied, "It's better than 3,500."

"Och, for a 3,500 house, I'd dress in a [expletive deleted]."

"Well," he interrupted, "that's exactly where you are dressing!"

Crazy Quilt, a rowdy, uproarious comedy, was the subject of a vehement condemnation by the preacher at the old First Presbyterian Church downtown. Imagine his rage when, on another occasion, a very famous actress drunkenly stumbled into his vestry. Knowing only that she was to play in a big, old church in Nashville, the inebriated thespian chose the first one she came across and demanded the astonished reverend's help in finding her dressing room. The story went that the good gentleman roused himself from his shocked stupor to reply, "Madame, you are dreadfully mistaken."

"This ish a church, ain't it?" she supposedly slurred. Assuring her it was, but not the one she sought, he sent her on her unsteady way to the Ryman, where Naff did not refuse the sanctuary of *her* church.

Two other actresses caused headlines while in Nashville. Tallulah Bankhead held court in the tiny backstage area after one appearance and alternately charmed and shocked the fans and reporters who crowded around her. Later, after another appearance at the Ryman, she interrupted a cocktail party at the home of a local society leader. Angered by what she believed was vindictive upstaging by her hostess, Bankhead turned a hose on her and the other guests.

On March 30, 1938, during a stirring performance by Helen Hayes in *Victoria Regina*, the first lady of the American theatre strode to the edge of the stage to deliver lines. Behind her the cast froze in their places when suddenly a curtain ripped from its moorings and, narrowly missing the star, dumped years of accumulated dust and debris on the cast. But, with regal aplomb, Hayes continued on.

Because of its history, its manager, and even its appearance, the Ryman often became a target. Writing in 1935, Herbert Drake of the *New York Herald Tribune* spiced his account of Fanny Brice's performance in the Ryman with a few words about the primitive hall and its immoderately eccentric manager. Naff never forgave him either slight and later blamed his article for inspiring the patronizing comments in actress Katharine Cornell's autobiography. Cornell recalled that on her visits she watched Naff distribute tickets from a shoebox (it was actually a shirt box) on the streets of Nashville. She said that Naff snacked on bananas as she walked the streets selling tickets, and whenever someone asked for a ticket, she found it "perhaps in the box, but more likely in her hair, or her cuff,

WSM radio's Snooky Lanson interviews Bob Hope and Doris Day on the day of their 1949 Ryman appearances.

Grand Ole Opry Archives

or her sweater pocket." In 1958, Tyrone Power gave a press conference after a performance in the Ryman and criticized the city for not having an adequate theatre for actors to practice their craft. Others such as Amelita Galli-Curci, Fritz Kreisler, and John McCormack, praised the acoustics without dwelling on the discomforts.

Bob Hope brought Doris Day and Les Brown and His Band of Renown with him in 1949 and broke all records for attendance and receipts at the Ryman. The comedian opened his show by announcing "What an amazing garage this is! What time do the bats fly out?" Describing the building as an intimate old place, he asked if he could have it when it fell down, but he begged the management not to take off the bandages until he had gotten out.

Hope enjoyed his experience so much that the next day from New York he issued a press release gently poking fun at "America's most picturesque institution." Retelling the story about Captain Ryman pouring all his liquor into the Cumberland River at the time of his conversion, Hope said, "Les Brown's band heard about it and, before we could stop them, they had on their diving trunks."

What Hope had to say about Nashville's famed Ryman enjoyed wide circulation: "It's also Katharine Cornell's favorite theatre and the audiences sure do love her. In fact, before I stepped out on the stage, they were laying eight to five I'd never make as good a Juliet as she.

"In 1914, Mrs. Elsie [*sic*] Naff, the manager, mortgaged her home to bring John McCormack here. Of course, in those days she could have gotten Crosby for the same money.

"I wondered what all those ropes were on the stage for. Then I found out that when Caruso sang here, before he got the first note out, they had to fasten the building down.

"And I loved working [there]. The first balcony almost completely circles the theatre and it's wonderful to have the audience all around you. Naturally every now and then I got that trapped feeling.

"But it was really a sellout and people were sitting on anything they could find. One woman complained when the manager gave her something to sit on. Halfway through the show she discovered it was her husband."

A program release announces the Opry's move to Ryman Auditorium.

WSM Special Collection, Vanderbilt University Library

III. The Opry House

Only four blocks away from Lula Naff's flourishing Ryman, another Nashville institution was growing in prominence. On October 5, 1925, radio station WSM began broadcasting from its Seventh and Union Street studios on the fifth floor of the headquarters of its parent company, the National Life and Accident Insurance Company. The radio station took its call letters from the insurance company's motto, "We Shield Millions," and boasted a talented staff of performers, writers, announcers, and engineers. Standouts included station founder Edwin W. Craig; genius engineer John H. "Jack" DeWitt, Jr.; and announcer and program director George Dewey Hay. In 1924, Hay, who went by the moniker, "The Solemn Old Judge," had been voted "world's most popular radio announcer" in a readers' poll conducted by *Radio Digest* magazine. In a quest to obtain the best and brightest, WSM management hired Hay away from his post at Chicago's WLS radio, where he had been instrumental in founding the *WLS Barn Dance*, a radio show featuring down-home folksy music.

Nashville and its surrounding communities were a hotbed for the old-time string band and fiddle music that Hay loved. He took the opportunity to showcase that music, which he labeled "down to earth for the earthy," on November 28, 1925, when WSM pianist, Eva Thompson Jones, brought her 77-year-old uncle to the station. Uncle Jimmy Thompson was a championship old-time fiddler who claimed he could play around 375 different tunes and liked to boast that he could "fiddle the taters off the vine."

Thompson launched his performance with "Tennessee Wagoner," and then began taking requests from listeners via telephone and telegram. Requests and praise for the old-time tunes poured into the station from people listening in that Saturday night, and Uncle Jimmy was back next week by popular demand.

The Saturday night "barn dance" programming immediately became a regular feature. An article in *The Tennessean* from December 1925, announced that "due to the recent revival in the popularity of the old familiar tunes, WSM has arranged to have an hour or two of them every Saturday night."

WSM aired a number of original programs in addition to the barn dance, but it was also a member of the National Broadcasting Company network. In December 1927, a classical program, "National Symphony Orchestra," conducted by Dr. Walter Damrosch, the celebrated leader of the New York Symphony, preceded the regular barn dance show. Nashville had already heard him conduct several times, and it was always in Ryman Auditorium. His orchestra had been one of the earliest to perform in the newly completed Tabernacle in the 1890s, and he was well known to the people of Nashville.

Hay recalled that on one fortuitous December night, as he and the barn dance musicians waited to kick off the show,

> The monitor in our Studio B was turned on, so that we would have a rough idea of the time which was fast approaching. At about five minutes before eight, your reporter called for silence in the studio. Out of the loudspeaker came the correct, but accented voice of Dr. Damrosch and his words were something like this: "While most artists realize there is no place in the classics for realism, nevertheless I am going to break one of my rules and present a composition by a young composer from Iowa, who sent us his latest number, which depicts the onrush of a locomotive."

After the performance, Dr. Damrosch signed off, and Hay was on the air. "We paid our respects to Dr. Damrosch and said something like this: 'Friends, the program which just came to a close was devoted to the classics. Dr. Damrosch told us that it was generally agreed that there is no place in the classics for realism. However, from here on out for the next three hours we will present nothing but realism.... It will be down to earth for the earthy.'"

He then introduced harmonica virtuoso DeFord Bailey, who played his own composition inspired by the sound of a train, the "Pan American Blues." After he had finished, Hay stepped to the microphone and uttered words that still reverberate in the national musical consciousness: "For the past hour we have been listening to music taken largely from Grand Opera, but from now on we will present 'The Grand Ole Opry.'" Thus WSM found an "official" name for what has become the world's longest continuously running radio show, broadcast on Saturday nights since 1925.

With the Grand Ole Opry, WSM had a growing hit on its hands. When fans attending the show grew so numerous as to block the corridors, Edwin W. Craig, an official with National Life, suggested letting them into the studio. Not only would this free the halls, but also the crowd's enthusiasm would add to the program's immediacy. Hoping to turn a problem into a boon, National Life built Studio C to hold 500 spectators. Before long, however, officials of the insurance company were complaining that so many people spilled out of the auditorium studio to clog the corridors that their offices were almost unreachable. The insurance company executives gave Hay an ultimatum: either broadcast the Grand Ole Opry without a studio audience or find a new venue. By that time, the audience was an integral part of the show, and Hay could not imagine carrying on without one.

So, in October 1934, the Opry began a series of moves that led it first to the Hillsboro Theatre (now the Belcourt Theatre), a location that quickly proved inadequate for the crowds. The Opry packed up, and in June 1936 it moved across the Cumberland River to the old Dixie Tabernacle on

Fatherland Street in East Nashville. There, spectators shuffled through the sawdust on the floor to sit on rough, splintery benches to hear such groups as the Fruit Jar Drinkers and the Gully Jumpers and to watch the antics of Sarie and Sallie. Some of the luckier ones were there the night a young man from East Tennessee, Roy Acuff, first appeared with his Smoky Mountain Boys and sang "The Great Speckled Bird."

The well-to-do homeowners in the otherwise quiet Edgefield neighborhood eventually demanded that the Opry take its parking problems, its raucous patrons, and its loud music elsewhere; so the Opry moved out of the Dixie Tabernacle in 1939.

Beginning in July of 1939, War Memorial Auditorium, an elegant neoclassical hall built in 1925 in downtown Nashville directly across from the National Life Building, was the Opry's next home. Roy Acuff recalled that he and his band would tune up and dress in the insurance headquarters building and then walk across to the Auditorium when it was time to perform. WSM decided that it had to control the crowds in some way and began charging a 25-cent entrance fee for the first time in 1939. But the fans still came in greater and greater numbers, and Grant Turner, who joined WSM as an Opry announcer in 1944, said, "They brought with them their chewing tobacco and gum and pocket knives to leave their initials in the War Memorial's fine leather seats." Three thousand and more came each week, and the wear and tear on War Memorial Auditorium led to a polite but firm request that the Opry find another home. The show found its next home just five blocks away in a venue that would rise to worldwide fame alongside its new tenant.

A short article in *The Tennessean* on June 5, 1943 stated, "The Grand Ole Opry, Saturday night radio show of Station WSM, will be staged hereafter at Ryman Auditorium, starting tonight, instead of at the War Memorial Building as previously, it was announced yesterday by Harry Stone, station manager." The Opry, which at that time prided itself on a hillbilly image and deemed its onstage antics "a good-natured riot," was not the sort of entertainment favored by L.C. Naff.

Roy Acuff and his Smoky Mountain Boys perform on the Opry in the 1940s. Left to right: Lon Wilson, Roy Acuff, Jimmie Riddle, Pete "Bashful Brother Oswald" Kirby, Velma Smith

John Hood photograph, Grand Ole Opry Archives

But a reliable, regular tenant—and one whose parent company's leaders were also members of the Auditorium Improvement Company—could not be turned away. A contract signed by National Life and the Auditorium Improvement Company to lease "Ryman Auditorium to the Grand Ole Opery [*sic*] for 52 consecutive Saturday nights" began on June 5, 1943, with National Life paying $100 per Saturday night, exempting one night in November from the lease because of a prior concert commitment. Naff's first mention of the Opry in her regular correspondence to her friend Francis Robinson was a complaint that country music fans had begun blocking her doorways. It was something Naff must have learned to tolerate, because ardent Opry fans would continue forming long lines to block the Ryman's doorways for decades to come.

The Opry's move to the Ryman coincided with an event that Harry Stone, longtime station manager of WSM, called one of the "things which more firmly established country music as a form of entertainment than anything else." In the fall of 1938, the William Esty Agency had secured the R.J. Reynolds Tobacco Company as a sponsor for a segment of the Opry on WSM. Less than a year later, the "Prince Albert Opry" began to broadcast over several NBC network affiliates in the Southeast. But on October 9, 1943, that program, the thirty minutes sponsored by Prince Albert Smoking Tobacco and now originating from the Ryman, expanded from 63 to 129 stations on a coast-to-coast NBC hookup. The Ralston Purina Company, impressed by the success of Prince Albert, contracted that same year to sponsor another thirty minutes through stations affiliated with NBC in the South and Southwest. Thus in the very year of its move into the Auditorium, the Opry spread the name "Ryman" nationwide.

Four years later, a WSM representative stood before the U.S. Federal Communications Commission Clear Channel hearing (which would clear the station for continued long-distance broadcasting during nighttime hours), arguing that the station's 50,000 watts "should not be curtailed." In defense of the station, he characterized "the Opry's tremendous enterprise" and gave a good description of what the move into the Ryman had entailed

> Far beyond our original plans for the program, the Grand Ole Opry has become a national institution. Let me briefly illustrate what I mean. We rent on an annual basis the largest auditorium in Middle Tennessee, in which we have installed complete studio facilities (control room, rehearsal rooms, public address system, floodlights, stage props, etc.). To handle the enormous crowds, we employ thirty-seven firemen, policemen, ushers, ticket sellers, stage hands, and electricians. This number, added to the number of performers,

Red Foley, Minnie Pearl, and Rod Brasfield, stars of the NBC Prince Albert Grand Ole Opry broadcast, watch from the wings.
Grand Ole Opry Archives

gives us a total of 152 people in all. The talent costs alone on the Grand Ole Opry is [*sic*] $1,500 per week.

The Ryman had, at this time, 3,574 seats, but not all of them could be used because the pillars obstructed sight lines to the stage. *The Tennessean* reported in an article three weeks after the move into the Ryman that, as large as it was, the Ryman might not be big enough for the fans who "formed in lines more than a block long an hour and a half before opening."

War Memorial Auditorium seated roughly 2,200 people. With the move into the Ryman, the Opry now afforded another thousand or so an opportunity to see the show each Saturday night. Minnie Pearl noted a direct correlation between the move to the Ryman and the "beginning of the explosion of country music." She cited the tent shows, which had begun to carry Opry stars to small towns throughout the South and Midwest in 1940, as one of the reasons for the explosion. "I was aware that things had changed when we moved into the Ryman," she said.

Minnie Pearl saw additional reasons why the Opry at the Ryman changed from a popular show to a national sensation. Because the move occurred during wartime and more and more soldiers made up its audience in the Ryman, the Opry took on new meaning for thousands of homesick, sometimes frightened young men. Times were propitious for spreading country music, and that is just what those soldiers did with their guitars and memories of nights at the Ryman.

Minnie Pearl also thought that the Opry was very successful in attracting outstanding talent to add to its already glittering roster. Uncle Dave Macon, the Opry's first big star, and Roy Acuff, the Opry's newest and brightest star, both moved into the Ryman along with the show. Others on those wartime programs included Bill Monroe, Ernest Tubb, Pee Wee King, Eddy Arnold and, of course, Minnie Pearl. Roy Acuff's mounting fame through personal appearances on the road and through his movie roles fed the flames of the Opry's renown. As he said,

> I didn't miss appearing on the Opry if I could help it. I just had to get in here for that Saturday night Opry. I would like to play somewhere like Myrtle Beach, South Carolina, on a Friday night and be in here on Saturday. I'd get in here maybe three or four o'clock in the afternoon, and go right on to the Auditorium, and my wife would meet me with my clothes, and I'd leave after the Opry and go back on the road.

WSM became a clear-channel station in 1928 and had constructed a new 50,000 watt transmitter that went online in 1932, blasting a signal that covered most of the continental United States and parts of Canada and Mexico. The Grand

Ole Opry's massive listening audience began to attract non-Nashville based touring acts for guest appearances on the show. One such act gaining nationwide exposure was Bob Wills and His Texas Playboys, whose song "San Antonio Rose" was the best-selling record of 1939. One of his guest appearances at the Opry caused an incident that Minnie Pearl described best:

> Bob Wills was young and handsome in that devil-may-care sort of way. When he did all that Texas hollering, that "Ah-haaa," some of the ladies would go all to pieces. He was the first person to park a bus in front of the Ryman, and what a sight they were coming out of it. He and the Playboys and San Antonio Rose all dressed in white cowboy outfits. Well, as you know, the Ryman has that semicircular balcony that curves around over the wings of the stage, and one of the ladies up there could not control herself when she saw Bob Wills. She stood up, started to shout, and fell out of the balcony directly onto the stage—a real showstopper since they had to stop and pick her up.

She said that retelling the story reminded her of a routine she did with Rod Brasfield, who told her, "Miss Minnie, I shot my dog."

"Why?" asked Minnie, "Was he mad?"

"Well, he wasn't very happy about it," replied Brasfield.

So, when people asked her if the lady who fell out of the balcony was hurt by the fall, Miss Minnie always answered, "Well, it didn't help her any."

Bob Wills, however, had as much impact on the Opry as he did on his fans. He brought his amplified fiddles with him, an innovation that caused Judge Hay to have heartburn and that caused Roy Acuff to tell Minnie Pearl, "They goin' to ruin the Opry." But in actuality, electric guitars had already invaded the Ryman when Pee Wee King's Golden West

Cowboys and Ernest Tubb and His Texas Troubadours used them. One other story persists about Wills's appearance. It has been repeated widely that he brought the first snare drum onto the stage but that Opry officials made him hide it behind a curtain. Actually, Pee Wee King's group probably was the first to use drums at the Opry, but whether they were first hidden and then banished remains in question. In an interview with author Chet Hagan for his history of the Opry, E.W. Wendell, then chief executive officer of Opryland USA, Inc., called the story about hiding the drums another of the "old tales around here." The issue of electric instruments and drums would persist for decades. Herman Crook scorned those who used them, and Roy Acuff thought they were "too loud" and "not pure."

New names began to be heard at the Opry after its move to the Ryman. The year of the move, Eddy Arnold left his role as vocalist in Pee Wee King's group and struck out as a solo artist. In 1944, Lester Flatt joined Bill Monroe's band. Also, as Minnie Pearl recalled fondly, Rod Brasfield joined the Ralston Purina network program that year, and Whitey Ford, the Duke of Paducah, appeared as the comic on the Prince Albert program. Brasfield got a rousing ovation after his first performance at the Ryman because, Minnie Pearl said, of his natural comedic talent. "There was this little man on the stage with his suit too big and his hat mashed up in his pants and his rubber face telling jokes with perfect timing. Working with Rod those 10 years in the Ryman is one of the most wonderful things that ever happened to me."

In 1945, Opry star Bill Monroe, leader of a string band named the Blue Grass Boys (a nod to Monroe's native state of Kentucky), began putting together the group of musicians that would give birth to a new genre of American music.

In December of that year, innovative banjoist Earl Scruggs joined the Blue Grass Boys, and his dynamic three-finger picking style electrified audiences. Over the next year, with Lester Flatt on guitar and lead vocals, Monroe added Chubby Wise on fiddle and Howard Watts (a.k.a. "Cedric Rainwater") on bass. Featuring Bill Monroe on mandolin and

Bill Monroe (mandolin) is joined by members of his Blue Grass Boys band; Chubby Wise (fiddle), Lester Flatt (guitar) and Earl Scruggs (banjo). Scholars consider this lineup, with the addition of Howard Watts on bass, to be the group that originated the acoustic string music that would become known as bluegrass.

John Hood photograph, Grand Ole Opry Archives

vocals, with virtuoso instrumentals and Monroe's signature "high-lonesome sound," the group evolved a new musical style. It would become known as bluegrass music, in tribute to Monroe's pioneering group. Fittingly, one of the last big festivals held in Ryman Auditorium before the Opry moved out was a bluegrass "revival" in 1973 that was headlined by none other than Bill Monroe. Bluegrass maintains a powerful connection to the Ryman and the stage on which it was born.

In late April 1946, Red Foley, who brought along a young guitar player named Chet Atkins, took over the Prince Albert Show. Grandpa Jones, the Willis Brothers, and Lonzo and Oscar also joined the Opry in 1946. The year 1947 saw Opry entertainers perform for the first time in Washington, D.C.'s Constitution Hall and New York City's

Carnegie Hall, an occasion that prompted Ernest Tubb's often repeated remark about the latter room, "This place'd hold a lot of hay." The contrast between the grandeur of Carnegie Hall and the Ryman's rough-hewn hominess was not lost on country performers, who, according to Minnie Pearl, began to appreciate the tradition and warmth of Ryman Auditorium.

In 1948, Eddy Arnold left the Opry over salary disputes. He resented the show's strict requirements that performers appear every Saturday night with few exceptions, forcing them to play for scale on what was the most profitable night of the week for an artist. George Morgan, who had a crooning style of singing similar to Arnold's, came in to replace him on the roster. That same year Roy Acuff unsuccessfully ran for governor of Tennessee, and WSM began its Friday night version of the Opry, the *Friday Night Frolic*, in its studios. Little Jimmy Dickens remembered that his first night at the Ryman was also in 1948:

> Roy Acuff brought me to the Opry. The one thing I remember most about my first appearance at the Ryman was my lifelong dream of just going backstage. I had been in radio in different parts of the United States for ten years before I first came to the Opry as a guest, and I thought that I was ready for it until I stepped on the stage of the Ryman Auditorium. I realized how many greats had stood there, and wondered whether or not I was worthy to follow them, and my knees started knocking, and I felt like I was doing my first talent contest even though I had ten years' experience. The Ryman Auditorium has a feel about it that's different from any stage I've ever been on…. I don't know what it is, but there's just something about the Ryman Auditorium.

In 1949, one of the watermark events in country music history occurred on the Ryman's stage. The night of June 11,

Amongst the rigging and sandbags that raised and lowered the various sponsor backdrops, Ernest Tubb gets ready to hit the Opry stage.

Gordon Gillingham photograph, Grand Ole Opry Archives

1949, may have seemed like just another night at the Opry for the thousands of fans and the people who entertained them, until a tall, lanky farm boy ambled out to the microphone and launched into his version of "Lovesick Blues." Hank Williams stopped the show. Minnie Pearl said, "Everybody, me included, rushed to the wings of the stage," and Little Jimmy Dickens remembered that "there were so many encores that I lost count of 'em." Others say the number was six and that Red Foley had to calm the crowd by promising that Hank Williams would be heard again on the Opry.

Opry announcer Grant Turner said that he knew something momentous was happening that night: "The fans just didn't want to let him go. When Hank would work that stage, he would appear to be suspended in a blue haze, very much as if you had a coat hanger in his suit holding him up over the microphone. He just had that way of being totally relaxed, and he, being a Southerner and knowing his audiences so well, had that easygoing drawl in his voice and manner that made people love him so much." Turner also described Williams in moments of repose: "Hank had a way of sitting on a couch, all slumped down, and he would wind one foot around the other. He would cross his leg and hook that toe back around the other leg—all wound up like a corkscrew."

The early 1950s saw other bright additions to the Opry's growing constellation of stars. Hank Snow became the first Canadian Opry member in 1950, and Martha Carson, Ray Price, and Faron Young joined in 1952. When the Carter Family—Mother Maybelle, Helen, June, and Anita—joined the Opry in May 1950, bringing Chet Atkins as their guitarist, many fans felt much as Dottie West did when she heard them in the Ryman: "We all know it was built as a tabernacle, and I would cry sometimes when I heard Anita's pure, sweet voice in that old building. It was just like hearing an angel sing."

An angel of a different type also shared the stage with the Carter Family. Kitty Wells brought her number one hit, "It Wasn't God Who Made Honky Tonk Angels," to the Ryman in 1952, and paved the way for other women to join the Opry. Just as Roy Acuff was country music's king, Kitty Wells reigned as its queen.

Hank Williams left the Opry in 1952, and Webb Pierce arrived. The year 1953 brought Jumpin' Bill Carlisle, who remembered that he was "real nervous" to be playing in Ryman Auditorium. Among his early memories of the Ryman was "seeing all those hand fans in the summertime. Old-timey hand fans." Laughingly, he poked gentle fun at the newer Opry management: "That's one thing they should of thought about before they moved us out of the Ryman. They lost their sales on all them hand fans when they moved out to an air-conditioned building."

Del Wood, Marty Robbins, Jim Reeves, the Louvin Brothers, Jean Shepard, and Justin Tubb all joined the Opry roster in the early 1950s. In 1954 a nonmember made his only appearance: Elvis Presley. Among those who remember that one appearance is Justin Tubb, who took the young singer to

Opry favorite and country music legend Hank Williams performs at the Ryman with Chet Atkins on guitar.

Gerald Holly photograph, Grand Ole Opry Archives

his father's record shop afterwards, and Little Jimmy Dickens, who said,

> I certainly do remember his one and only
> performance on the Grand Ole Opry. I was
> very interested in Elvis. I had been hearing
> his records and "Blue Moon of Kentucky" was
> catching on, the old Bill Monroe song with the
> Elvis touch. His record was just getting real
> good and hot, and I'd been looking forward
> to hearing this young man. He came to the
> Ryman, and I was so anxious to see how
> the audience of the Grand Ole Opry would
> respond. Really, the response was not that
> good. Elvis didn't click at all on his first and
> only appearance. Our audience was there for
> the dyed-in-the-wool country music, and that's
> not exactly what Elvis was doing.

Skeeter Davis remembered Elvis musing aloud to her, "I wonder why they don't like me at the Opry, because Marty Robbins gets up there and does my songs and they love him."

Aside from "rockabilly," the Ryman saw other innovations in the early 1950s. By this time country and pop music had blended into a sound that made many songwriters and artists rich and famous. Recordings were even made in the Ryman itself. For example, whenever Castle Studios wanted to record Red Foley with orchestral accompaniment, they did it from the Auditorium. In an article for *The Journal of Country Music* (December 1978), music historian John Rumble explained that "On sessions taking place in the Ryman involving orchestra and/or background vocalists, the engineers kept their [disc] cutting lathe at the Tulane Hotel. They fed the electrical impulses from microphones at the Ryman through a telephone line rented for this purpose." Probably the earliest date for a recording session in the Ryman was the one on April 9, 1952, found by Rumble in the Castle Studio logbooks.

Anita Carter, Mother Maybelle Carter, Helen Carter, Ferlin Husky, Chet Atkins, Jean Shepard, Carl Smith, Minnie Pearl, the Collins Kids, Buddy Ebsen, June Carter, Earl Scruggs, Lester Flatt, and the Jordanaires appear on the Ralston Purina television show in 1955.

Gordon Gillingham photograph, Grand Ole Opry Archives

Television also came to the Ryman in 1955 with a network program, sponsored by Ralston Purina, airing the fourth week of every month, and featuring Grand Ole Opry stars alongside guests from across the entertainment spectrum, including Tony Bennett, Buddy Ebsen, and opera singer Marguerite Piazza. ABC's Grand Ole Opry show was broadcast live one hour before the Opry, which began at 8:00 p.m. In that way the producers used the Opry crowd as an audience for the broadcast. It required a tight turnaround and set strike because the television production featured elaborate themed sets, which were not part of the regular Opry show. Minnie Pearl remarked that

Purina seemed pleased with it, since they got to sell a lot of bulk feed for hogs and cows. They'd set those sacks there on the stage, and Roy and I had to sit on them sometimes for publicity shots. One time, some real smart ad-man decided to do a fan mail poll, and they asked Roy and I to make the pitch. Roy told all the people who were watching to write a card or letter and just to tell us that they were watching, not whether they liked the show or not. Well, they got so many cards and letters that they had to hire ten secretaries to handle them all. They divided them up into rural, urban, and suburban stacks, and found out that they were from the urban and suburban viewers. Well, Purina was trying to sell feed to the rural people, and so they cancelled the show.

Another early television show cited by former Opry Manager Hal Durham was a Christmas special for Martha White Flour, a loyal Opry sponsor that saw a dramatic growth in sales after it began advertising on the Grand Ole Opry. Through the next twenty years, television cameras became a routine fixture in the Ryman, with Arlene Francis, Dinah Shore and Jimmy Dean all shooting segments or episodes of their shows there, in addition to several syndicated country music shows produced by WSM-TV, and featuring performances by Grand Ole Opry stars.

The annual Country Music Association Awards would later be telecast from the Ryman, requiring many changes, including an extended temporary stage that projected over eight or nine rows of pews. The producers redecorated the stage to mask its more rustic aspects and hung white, starry lights throughout the area. The awards show was a success, and it was an annual event at the Ryman until it moved to the new Opry House.

Lester Flatt and Earl Scruggs (at the microphone) perform at Ryman Auditorium with (left to right) Paul Warren, Jake Tullock, and Josh Graves. In the right foreground, Opry announcer T. Tommy Cutrer contemplates his next remarks, and, in the left background, the ever-watchful Opry manager Vito Pellettieri makes sure things run smoothly as bassist Lightning Chance watches the show.

Gordon Gillingham photograph, Grand Ole Opry Archives

In 1955, Lula C. Naff retired as manager of the Ryman, and her assistant of four years, Harry Draper, took over the job. Road shows like *Oklahoma!* and *Back to Methuselah* continued to play the Ryman, as did musical stars like Pete Fountain and Duke Ellington. But the real business of the Ryman had become the Opry.

There were changes in Opry management as well. Dee Kilpatrick took over from Jim Denny in 1956 as the Opry's general manager and as manager of WSM's Artist Services Bureau. He believed strongly that the Opry needed a mix of traditional entertainers and newer, younger stars to balance its appeal. To attract new fans, he brought in the Everly Brothers and Rusty and Doug Kershaw. Furthermore, he delighted the traditionalists by continuing the ban on drum kits ("symbols of rock and roll") on the Opry, but antagonized them at the same time by consolidating four of the original string bands into two groups, the Crook Brothers and the Fruit Jar Drinkers.

Johnny Cash's first Opry appearance in 1956 was a sensation. Carl Smith introduced him as "the brightest rising star in country music of America," and Minnie Pearl told the adoring crowd, "If I was thirty years younger and thirty pounds lighter, we'd be courting tonight." When he finished singing "I Walk the Line," the No. 2 song in the nation at the time, the crowd stood and roared its approval. Jimmy C. Newman and Stonewall Jackson joined Cash in becoming the newest cast members in 1956. Wilma Lee and Stoney Cooper and Porter Wagoner joined them in 1957, and a little girl from Sevierville, Tennessee, Dolly Parton, sang one song on the *Friday Night Frolic*. The Stoney Mountain Cloggers brought their versions of mountain dances to the stage in 1958. The last years of the 1950s brought other new talent to the Ryman: Don Gibson, Del Reeves, Skeeter Davis, Archie Campbell, and others.

But there were also painful times. Rod Brasfield died of a heart attack in 1958, and in 1959 the Opry's beloved stage manager Vito Pellettieri faced mandatory retirement. Every one of the Opry performers signed a petition asking WSM to allow him to remain, if not in his post as music librarian, then at least as Opry stage manager. Often called "the contrariest man alive," Pellettieri had for years turned the total confusion of Saturday nights on the Ryman stage into the "organized chaos" that was the Opry. WSM officials, overwhelmed by the entertainers' demands that he remain with the show, relented, and he continued to goad his "family" to give their best performances until his death on April 14, 1977, at age 87.

Hank Locklin and Bill Anderson both became regular performers in the early 1960s, and Patsy Cline and Loretta Lynn began appearing regularly. One need not be an Opry fan to realize the impact of these two women on the music industry. Certainly one of the saddest events in the Ryman's long history, a history that had seen memorial services for such men as Sam Jones, William McKinley, William Jennings Bryan,

Johnny Cash and The Tennessee Two (Marshall Grant and Luther Perkins) in a 1956 Opry appearance at the Ryman

Gordon Gillingham photograph, Grand Ole Opry Archives

Governor Austin Peay, and President Theodore Roosevelt, was the short interruption in the Opry on Saturday night, March 9, 1963, for a tribute to five of its entertainers who had died that week. Ott Devine, manager of the Grand Ole Opry, asked the audience to stand with the assembled performers that night for a silent prayer of tribute to Patsy Cline, Cowboy Copas, Hawkshaw Hawkins, and Randy Hughes, who had died in a tragic plane crash, and singer Jack Anglin, who had been killed

Patsy Cline, an Opry favorite, performs at Ryman Auditorium, where later her fellow performers would pay tribute to her and three others who died tragically in a plane crash in Camden, Tennessee.

Les Leverett photograph, Grand Ole Opry Archives

in a car accident on his way to the memorial service for Cline the day before. The Jordanaires then sang "How Great Thou Art," and the Opry resumed.

These were also important years in the history of the building itself. In 1961, the Ryman celebrated its seventieth birthday with a gala performance by the American Ballet Theatre under the musical direction of future Nashville Symphony maestro, Kenneth Schermerhorn. For that evening the old Tabernacle came alive with gaslights on its sidewalks, antique cars at its doorstep, and a red carpet and canopy covering its stairs. That same evening, some of the Opry's stars invaded Carnegie Hall for a rousing, sold-out performance. Despite their success, Dorothy Kilgallen, popular New York columnist, raised the ire of many an Opry lover when she referred to the visitors as "hicks from the sticks."

The Ryman still hosted conventions, revivals, sporting events (wrestling matches, for example), fine arts programs, and even an occasional livestock show. One of the earliest events in the Union Gospel Tabernacle had been a performance by the celebrated horse, Jim Key, but these later shows in the Ryman featured purebred cattle exhibitions. Grant Turner explained how the cattle got onto the stage: "They brought them in the back door. There was one entrance to the Opry House [the Ryman] that was probably used to bring in heavy equipment, and they could run those cattle down from the truck right through the door. Once inside the Opry House, they could lead them to the stage through a series of ramps. Those cattle could walk on those ramps with no problem at all right to the stage. They probably put a tarp over the stage and then straw over that to have their cattle show."

Because of competition from newer local venues and the scarcity of good shows, manager Draper was unable to give Nashville the same kind of music and theatre that Naff had presented in the 1930s. Yet he too leapt to the defense of the Ryman as a home for the Opry when a letter in *The Tennessean* suggested that it was an inappropriate locale. In his rejoinder, Draper maintained that "much of" the Opry's "fabulous appeal, which is international," would disappear in any other location. He believed that the Opry and the Ryman were perfectly compatible.

National Life got the opportunity to show that they shared his belief when they bought the Ryman from its board on September 27, 1963 for $207,500. Negotiations for another long-term lease had fallen through, and the insurance company decided that, rather than pay $20,000 a year in rent, it made better sense to buy the building. National Life immediately renamed it the "Grand Ole Opry House."

WSM set about quickly to remodel the building and to make repairs, some necessitated by a ruling from Actors' Equity Association that prohibited its union members from working shows there. Actors from a touring company of *Luther* had complained that cables stretched across the backstage area were a safety hazard and that the building was "unsanitary." WSM, which had just spent more than $25,000 on improvements, negotiated a reversal of the order with Actors' Equity. After fire marshals deemed the building structurally sound and in good repair, the union rescinded its ban.

The growing number of people who wanted to see the *Friday Night Frolic* finally forced WSM to move the weekly event to the Ryman in 1964. Again, Studio C had become too cramped. Roy Acuff explained, "They had to move it. I'd tell people to come see it, and they wouldn't be able to get in the studio. They'd blame me and so I was glad they moved it on over to the Ryman." In the transfer, the *Frolic* became the *Friday Night Opry*.

The fans forced another alteration to the schedule in 1966. The summer months saw such vast numbers of people who wanted tickets that the Grand Ole Opry began Saturday matinee performances to accommodate its fans. On one July weekend 15,000 people had tried to get tickets for one of the shows, and the Opry had been forced to stage a late performance from 12:30 p.m. until 2 a.m. By early July, all reserved tickets through September 1 had already been sold out.

The year 1966 also saw an inspired addition to the Ryman's appearance, one that many might assume had been a part of the building since construction. Stained glass panes were added to the arched windows along the north side on both floors of the auditorium. Sunlight streaming through the red, green, blue, and yellow panes bathes the auditorium in a beautiful warm light, and the stained glass is perfectly at home in the old Tabernacle.

New stars and acts such as Marion Worth, Ernie Ashworth, the Browns, Dottie West, Willie Nelson, and the Osborne Brothers appeared continuously between 1963 and

Dolly Parton and Porter Wagoner sing one of the duets for which they were beloved by their fans.

Les Leverett photograph, Grand Ole Opry Archives

1964. In 1964, the Opry listed fifty-five star acts and a total cast of more than 100 performers. But that same year, the Opry lost some of its biggest attractions. Jim Reeves died in a plane accident. Additionally, because they failed to appear on the then-required twenty-six shows a year, the Opry dropped eleven stars from its roster: Kitty Wells, Ray Price, George

Morgan, Don Gibson, Billy Grammer, Johnnie Wright, the Jordanaires, Faron Young, Ferlin Husky, Justin Tubb, and Stonewall Jackson.

The last years of the 1960s saw other artists added as members, including Tex Ritter, Bobby Bare, Bob Luman, Connie Smith, Jack Greene, Charlie Walker, Jeannie Seely, the Four Guys, and last but not least Dolly Parton.

In the early seventies, the Opry added performers who had the good fortune to spend part of their careers in a building that had become synonymous with country music. The group included Tom T. Hall, David Houston, Barbara Mandrell, Jerry Clower, and Jeanne Pruett, who proudly pointed out that she was "the last singing artist to join the Grand Ole Opry while it was still at Ryman Auditorium." On a tragic note, however, beloved performer David "Stringbean" Akeman was killed in a grisly assault after returning home from the Opry in 1973, the year before the move into the new Opry House.

Over the years, the Opry had brought other radio broadcasts and events to the Ryman, including the Country Music Disc Jockeys Convention beginning in 1952 and Grand Ole Gospel Time, a live gospel music show hosted by Reverend Jimmie Snow, Hank Snow's son, which followed the Friday Night Opry from 1972 until 1994. In addition, the Auditorium was the scene for beauty contests, talent shows, and marriages. "Bashful" Brother Oswald was married at the Ryman, and he and Roy Acuff occasionally served as "best men" for couples who wanted a lifetime memory of being married on the stage that hosted the Opry. But it was a former Opry member, and surprisingly, one who had been banished from the Ryman stage, who would bring a production that would introduce the "Mother Church of Country Music," as the Ryman was coming to be known, to a new, ever-widening audience.

Johnny Cash and the Opry parted company in 1965. In his autobiography, *Man in Black*, Cash described that night in the Ryman, a night when he began to realize that pills were taking a devastating toll on his life.

The Johnny Cash Show brought the Man in Black back to the Ryman for what was the largest television production staged there to that date.

Sid O'Berry photograph, Grand Ole Opry Archives

> The band kicked off a song, and I tried to take the microphone off the stand. In my nervous frenzy I couldn't get it off. Such a minor complication in my mental state was enough to make me explode in a fit of anger. I took the mike stand, threw it down, then dragged it along the edge of the stage, popping 50 or 60 footlights. The broken glass shattered all over the stage and into the audience.

Ott Devine, then Opry manager, quietly told Cash backstage that the Opry would no longer be able to use him.

Despite his dismissal from the Opry, Cash's reverence for the Ryman continued. He never forgot the warm welcome of the audience that first night in 1956, and he never forgot the hall itself. Years later, when he could call the shots, he demanded that ABC's *The Johnny Cash Show*, which premiered June 7, 1969, be taped in the Ryman. Cash boldly featured artists from across the American musical spectrum: country, jazz, rock, and folk. The eclectic line-up of guest performers included Bob Dylan, Neil Young, Louis Armstrong, Joni Mitchell, and Ray Charles.

At the time, Cash told a reporter for *The Tennessean*, "I love that old building. I love the feeling it gives me, and I love the people." Johnny Cash did not want a Hollywood studio or a Hollywood audience for his variety show; he wanted the real thing and knew that he would find it only in Nashville at Ryman Auditorium. His production staff, some thirty strong, moved to Nashville. An acoustical engineer from Texas advised them how best to adapt the Ryman for the program, and they converted an old tavern across the alley from the Auditorium's back door into a series of offices and dressing rooms.

For each taping they parked their trailer, jammed with studio equipment and technical material, at the back door, and they had scenery and props built in a nearby workroom and brought over to the Ryman. Before the programs could be taped, the staff had to build an extension onto the old stage over which they laid special flooring. All of their labor lasted only as long as the taping, because the Ryman had to be restored to its everyday appearance before the following Friday night. The whole process took over ten hours, but the result was a show that resonated with authenticity and made its host, with his weekly introduction, "Hello, I'm Johnny Cash," a household name. Johnny Cash knew instinctively what others found out slowly but surely—that the Auditorium always becomes an important part of the show.

Long lines stretching down the street were a familiar sight on Friday and Saturday nights as fans flocked to see the Grand Ole Opry.

Les Leverett photograph, Grand Ole Opry Archives

IV. Mother Church: Nights at the Opry

All who were part of the Grand Ole Opry at the Ryman during those years had colorful tales to tell. Most can vividly recall, for example, scores of people standing under the hot summer sun, four to eight abreast and forming lines stretching for blocks on some days. All were waiting for tickets to the Opry, and some of them would wait three to four hours to get into the Ryman.

Porter Wagoner never forgot the sight:

> I came in from the road one Saturday morning
> and got off the bus and started home. I drove
> up Broad Street and saw people lined up six
> abreast all the way from the Ryman around
> the corner to Broad. For a whole block down
> Broad! Just waiting to get tickets to see the
> Grand Ole Opry. This was at 6:30 a.m.
> I remembered that I'd waited in line, too,
> when I was fourteen years old. How important
> country music could be to these fans that
> they would wait for five hours just to get
> tickets! I can't express how I felt when I saw
> that happen.

Souvenir sellers hawked their wares to the crowd. Ushers kept fans in line with ropes and bullhorns, and evangelical preachers (fitting, given the Ryman's roots in religion) shouted at them and passed out pamphlets. The fans, dressed in everything from overalls and work boots to Sunday clothes, stood patiently, expectantly. Grant Turner often saw a man selling "rooster whistles," and on Saturday afternoons downtown Nashville sometimes sounded like a chicken coop when small boys tried out this ingenious toy. Occasionally winos asked people in line for some spare change and then shuffled away.

By the evening, parking was nonexistent around the Ryman. Every manner of vehicle, Cadillacs and buses for the stars, Fords and Chevys for the fans, fought for space throughout the neighborhood. Turner described how enterprising truck owners in small towns loaded up their flat beds with people and drove into Nashville on Saturdays. The ride back in the 1940s probably cost about the same as a ticket to the Opry.

Heartbroken fans who could not get in stood on the outside and looked through the windows that ticketholders, who were desperate for a little cool air, had flung open. So hot was the Ryman in July that Roy Acuff said, "It made my head swim to see all those hand fans a-pumpin' out there. I'd get so dizzy I'd have to close my eyes."

Minnie Pearl hungrily recalled the box lunches the fans brought, often containing baked ham and fried chicken and potato salad, which they washed down with soft drinks from the Ryman's concession stands. Infants in arms got their meals, too; it was not unusual to see mothers nursing their children during performances.

On the stage the Opry lovers saw dancers, singers, comics, announcers, and stagehands in a frenzy of activity, because after all, this was a radio show and had to keep to a fairly rigid timetable. When asked if it seemed like organized chaos, Jeannie Seely retorted, "More like 'accidental organization,' if you ask me." Backdrops advertising Martha White Flour, R.C. Cola, Jefferson Island Salt, or Prince Albert Tobacco flew up and down at the appointed time. Differently colored footlights illuminated a quick set change to a farmhouse. June Carter liked to sit in a rocking chair to

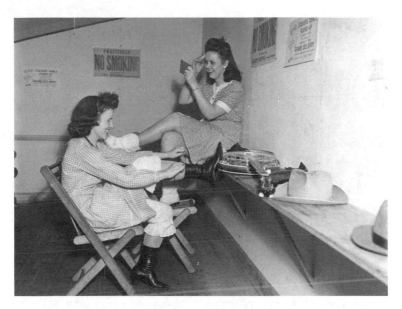

Rachel Veach and Velma Williams prepare for their set with Roy Acuff's band in one of the backstage dressing areas.

John Hood photograph, Grand Ole Opry Archives

enjoy the rest of the show when she was not performing. Ben Smathers and the square dancers took their hard-earned breaks on benches on the left side of the stage. People milled around, gossiping, laughing, and "cutting up." Hank Snow got so hot sometimes that he would twirl his handkerchief in front of his face for a little fresh air, and Porter Wagoner brought two suits because one was always sweat drenched by the time he finished his first show.

Comics kept the crowds in stitches, especially in the 1940s and 1950s. Roy Acuff's band had a routine in which one member unfurled a shirt stuffed into his pants some 20 feet across the stage. Lonzo and Oscar mugged and horsed around, whether it was their spot or not.

The best seats probably were in the balcony, and lucky was the sideman who had his girlfriend in the section over the wings so that he could join her between sets. "Unlucky," according to Jerry Rivers, fiddler for Hank Williams's Drifting

Little Jimmy Dickens goes to great heights to reach a bevy of fans. The balcony, which wrapped around to the back wall, provided seats directly over the sides of the stage.

Gordon Gillingham photograph, Grand Ole Opry Archives

Cowboys, "was the star who had his wife and girlfriend up there at the same time."

Backstage the Crook Brothers, the Gully Jumpers, and the Fruit Jar Drinkers often got together for impromptu jams in one of the dressing rooms. A banjo player might have had to stand out in the hall to try out his new material. Sometimes, Jan Howard recalled, "It would get so crowded back there that you had to leave in plenty of time or you'd miss your spot." The men had primitive, cramped dressing rooms; the women had only a bathroom.

The bathroom is still a sore point for some "country women." Barbara Mandrell described it for Chet Hagan: "You know what I recall most about the old Ryman? It's dressing and getting made-up and all in the toilet, which was the women's dressing room. That was really close, and warm and friendly, sharing that crowded space with Loretta Lynn and Connie Smith and Dolly Parton and Jeannie Seely."

Many things happened in that ladies' room. Jan Howard had a run-in with Patsy Cline that ended in a warm friendship. An innocent Skeeter Davis learned some of the seamier secrets of show biz. Dottie West saw "girls sitting on the floor trying to get dressed, sitting on some other things trying to get dressed too. I'm not going to tell you where my spot was, but, anyway, it was always a mighty full room." Too Slim of Riders In The Sky once asked Jeannie Seely, "With virtually no dressing area, how did they handle men and women backstage?" She laughed and said, "That's how all the older members of the Opry got to know each other." Backstage was no place for modesty.

When entertainers left the building, they found their fans waiting. If they were only going over to Tootsie's Orchid Lounge for a drink or Linebaugh's for something to eat, they stopped and chatted for a minute. Porter Wagoner and Dolly Parton ran into a logjam of fans one night as they made their way hurriedly to their bus. He recalled,

> After our spot we had to leave immediately
> to head for a matinee show in Pennsylvania
> the next day. When we got out the back door,
> there was just fans everywhere, unbelievable.
> This was just after Dolly and I had won the
> CMA [Country Music Association] Award at
> the Ryman Auditorium [1970] for Best Duet of
> the Year, and she and I were very popular with
> the fans. I would have loved to have stopped
> and signed autographs, but we couldn't do it
> and make our commitment to the show. So, I
> told the people when we came out, "Now wait
> a minute. We can't sign autographs, because
> we are in a rush." I explained about the next
> day's show and said, "It's not fair for us to sign
> one or two when there are so many of you, so I
> hope that y'all will understand and forgive us."
> Well, one lady just kept after us; she followed
> us and kept on saying, "Just sign mine, just

sign my autograph book." I told her, "Lady, I can't just sign yours. It wouldn't be right for me to sign yours and not sign anyone else's." She pestered us all the way to the bus. When I opened the door and stepped inside, we heard her say, "Well, I'm sure glad I voted for Conway and Loretta last year."

Local characters frequented the area around the Ryman. Jerry Rivers talked about one man nicknamed "City View," who lived in a cardboard shack on the roof of Tootsie's. Hal Durham remembered a man called "Up-the-Alley-O'Malley." Roy Acuff was known as an "easy mark" for the panhandlers, and Ernest Tubb even set up an account at one of the neighborhood restaurants for the winos. None of them ever used that account. Stars, fans, and the down-and-out mingled and mixed at the Ryman's back door.

Something was always going on back there, according to Chet Atkins. Undiscovered songwriters, singers, and musicians begged for a chance to display their talents. Sometimes, as Jerry Rivers revealed, someone would oblige:

George Morgan and Robert Lunn (Roy Acuff's "Talking Blues Boy") used to audition people out in the alley. There was an old outhouse out there with a corrugated tin roof, and people would be standing around in front of it. Some old boy would ask Mr. Acuff, "Roy, please just give me a chance to show you what I can do." And he'd tell 'em, "Well, son, you're just going to have to talk with Mr. Lunn. He's the boss around here." Then somebody would go tell Robert that he had an appointment out in the alley. He would come on out and ask the boy, "Well, what can you do?"

"I'm a singer." They were always singers.

"Can you dance?" Robert Lunn would ask. "We got plenty of singers, but we're always looking for somebody on the Opry that can dance."

"Well, yeah, I can learn to dance." And the first thing you know, they can dance, and they'd just whip into it. But Robert always told them, "I can't tell anything by that, you've got to be like you're on a stage."

In a minute, the tin roof on that old shanty would just be a rattlin.

The shenanigans did not stop at the back door. George Morgan was infamous for his practical jokes. In the days when Jerry Rivers played for Bill Monroe, Carl and Pearl Butler, and Cowboy Copas, he recalled that there just were not that many good steel guitar players around, "aside from Don Helms who was one of the very best." One of the novice players was in such a learning stage that he had a piece of masking tape on the neck of his guitar with the notes written on it. "So, Shot Jackson went out and peeled that tape up and moved it a fret," said Rivers. "And it worked out that the old boy played a fret sharp all night. He'd hear that it wasn't right, and he'd look down at the tape and it would still be in the same place." The other sidemen tried hard to hide their laughter.

Every night at the Opry was a special night, but for those fans who had driven miles and miles just to hear and to see Marty Robbins, there were special treats in store. Robbins in his later career developed a strong bond with his fans. One woman even tried to disrobe for him at the Ryman one night right in front of the stage, but Marty persuaded her otherwise. He liked to race cars on Saturdays and therefore preferred the latest time slot, 11:30 p.m., on the schedule. He usually kept going well after midnight when the other entertainers had already left for home or gone over to the Ernest Tubb Record Store for the Midnight Jamboree. After he finished playing and singing, he would sit on the edge of the stage and talk and visit with his fans. When the ushers finally had to close the

Marty Robbins signs autographs after the Opry show.
Les Leverett photograph, Grand Ole Opry Archives

Ryman, he would sometimes go out on the front steps and sign autographs until the wee hours of the morning. Hal Durham said, "He had to tip the street cleaner who couldn't get his work done for all the people waiting for a chance to talk with Marty."

The Opry regulars have their own vivid memories of performances by their friends and colleagues in Ryman Auditorium. Dolly Parton maintains that she did not know the meaning of the expressions "sex appeal" and "charisma" until she saw Johnny Cash on that stage. Porter Wagoner said that when he first went to the Ryman, Roy Acuff "had probably one of the best shows I'd ever seen in my life." Jeannie Seely remembered that the Osborne Brothers "just stopped me in my tracks" one night when they did "Kentucky." "I had only heard it on the radio and when I heard it in that auditorium, and they did the part where the music stops and they just do the harmony part, I could hear them breathe. I thought to myself, 'The Osborne Brothers even breathe in harmony!'"

Sonny Osborne, Bobby Osborne, and Dottie West are pictured with Opry manager Ott Devine on the night of their induction into the Opry cast—August 8, 1964.

Les Leverett photograph, Grand Ole Opry Archives

Dottie West made it a point to go up in the balcony to watch Marty Robbins. She described other special performances by Mother Maybelle Carter and Kitty Wells. Skeeter Davis looked forward to every performance by Loretta Lynn in the Ryman, because "…she just seems to epitomize the best kind of country singer." Bill Carlisle was there for Patsy Cline's and Jim Reeves's first nights, performances that impressed him, but it was Stringbean he associated most strongly with the Ryman.

Jan Howard, of course, recalled the legends—Bill Monroe, Minnie Pearl, Roy Acuff, and Ernest Tubb—when they appeared at the Ryman, but she also remembered fondly others who made the Opry happen: "Mr. Norris and Mr. Bell, the guards, and Vito [Pellettieri], the 'Grand Ole Man of the Grand Ole Opry,' as I called him." Norman Van Dame, a former guard at the new Opry House as well as the Ryman, stayed late

Loretta Lynn accepts the Country Song Roundup 1967 Favorite Female Artist Award from Opry announcer Grant Turner.

Les Leverett photograph, Grand Ole Opry Archives

one night to watch Stonewall Jackson record from the stage of the old Tabernacle. Hank Williams "wasn't one of my favorites," he added, "but I'll tell you what, it was a dream to hear Patsy Cline singing in that old building."

Grant Turner had an abundance of special memories: Brother Oswald playing the Dobro; Hank Snow and Porter Wagoner in their glittering Nudie Cohn–designed, or "Nudie," suits; the sad, sweet songs like "Molly Darling" by the Old Hickory Singers; Judge Hay blowing his steamboat whistle; June Carter and Johnny Cash showing up unexpectedly; Uncle Dave Macon twirling his banjo; Patsy Cline in a wheelchair after her automobile accident; DeFord Bailey making guest appearances; and even a wide-mouthed Joe E. Brown appearing in the touring production of *Harvey*.

For all these people, the Ryman was a place of magic and mystery, of tradition and spirituality, of warmth and hospitality. Yet by the late 1960s, looking back over the roughly

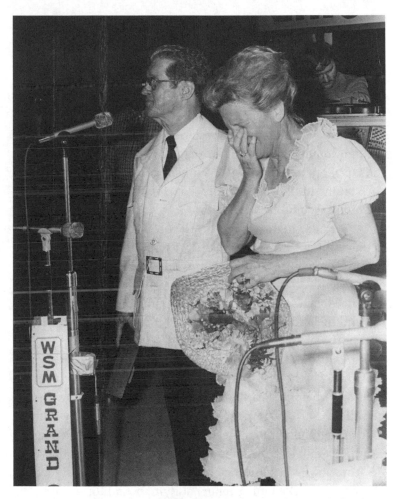

Roy Acuff is stoic as Minnie Pearl cries during the Opry's final Saturday night performance at the Ryman before moving to Opryland, March 9, 1974.

Jerry Bailey photograph, Grand Ole Opry Archives

thirty years in the Ryman, some felt that it was time for a change. Downtown had lost residents and thriving businesses to Nashville's growing suburbs, and the area surrounding the Ryman was filling in with pawn shops and peep shows, attracting a clientele that did not represent the family-friendly image that the Opry had always presented. The building itself, with no air conditioning, rudimentary dressing rooms, and bare-bones production facilities, became seen as inadequate in light of the growth of the country music industry and success of its superstars, who were accustomed to more comfortable accommodations. National Life executive, Irving Waugh, formally presented the idea of moving out of the Ryman in a 1968 company memorandum, stating his concerns: "I am of the opinion that if we don't move to modernize our concept of the Opry operation, we will eventually lose that which has been such an institution." The family that is the Opry had outgrown the building, and the Opry had to move on.

Friday night, March 15, 1974, was one of sorrowful anticipation for the Grand Ole Opry family. The next day they would be moving out of Ryman Auditorium to a new home at Opryland USA, and there were no plans for them ever to return. Most believed that the old Ryman could no longer sustain the hard use their fans gave it. It was to be a special occasion, with such stars as Porter Wagoner and Dolly Parton flying in just for the two nights. Most paid tribute to the Ryman that Friday night with their songs, their words, and even with their tears. Minnie Pearl, with eyes streaming, tried to reassure herself, saying, "It's going to be all right." The last thirty minutes of the program that night featured George Morgan, the Four Guys, Ray Pillow, Lonzo and Oscar, and Ernie Ashworth. When the last song had been sung and the radio announcer signed off, the Grand Ole Opry's tenure at Ryman Auditorium was over, at least for those listening on the radio.

Those in attendance that night took part in one final gospel sing of "Will the Circle Be Unbroken," led by Johnny Cash and June Carter. The prayerful song, sung in that rounded, shabby interior, offered closure to the Ryman's era as the Grand Ole Opry House but expressed hope that the building would have a future life.

The Ryman was open for daily tours after the Opry left in 1974, and little else. Many of the decorative windows were boarded up and the balcony was off-limits. Fans still made the pilgrimage to stand on the historic stage.

Grand Ole Opry Archives

V. The Ryman's Rebirth

The final notes of that night in 1974 echoed around the old Ryman Auditorium for twenty long years while downtown Nashville emptied out and languished. Once an icon of civic pride, the Ryman for many had become in the 1970s and 1980s a spent temple for a forgotten faith. Only one small relic of the Ryman moved on with the Grand Ole Opry.

Performers taking the stage at the new Grand Ole Opry House found an ever-present reminder of Ryman Auditorium and of all the legendary artists who had trod the well-worn boards there. During construction of the new facility, a section of the Ryman's oak stage flooring was removed, cut into a six foot circle, and inlaid front and center in the light maple stage floor at the Opry House. The circle of wood, a tangible representation of the connection between the Opry's past and future, became a magical place where contemporary artists feel a kinship with the greats who came before them.

However, while business boomed at the new Opry House and surrounding Opryland USA theme park, the Ryman seemed to have only a past. Instead of music or theatre presented by the world's great artists, the only sounds in the building were those of tourists communing with spirits or having their pictures made on the stage against the well-used Opry backdrop. But those admiring and knowing tourists kept making the pilgrimage, paying a dollar for a chance to be inside the Ryman's hallowed space. In a lean but steady way, they kept regard for the Ryman alive.

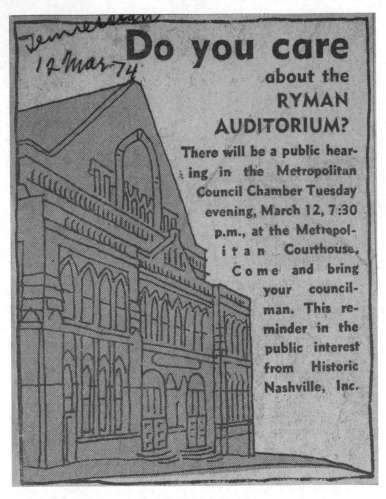

Advertisement for a rally held by local preservationists in support of saving the Ryman

The Tennessean

Unquestionably, the Mother Church was lucky to still be standing. While construction was underway on the new Opry House, a debate raged in Nashville over a question that today seems incomprehensible: Was the building, with its shabby, minuscule backstage, splintery pews, and hot humid air, simply used up? Should the aged structure be torn down? Initially, National Life officials took the position that the Ryman was beyond renovation, reasoning further that a refurbished theatre, buzzing with people on Friday and Saturday nights, would generate competition to its new upscale Grand Ole Opry House that was miles from downtown. Even Roy Acuff, the Grand Ole Opry's grand old man, thought the Ryman to be unsalvageable. He hated its heat and its ramshackle feeling, and he was in favor of an Opry management proposal to use the Ryman's bricks to construct the "Little Church of Opryland" inside Opryland USA.

The Ryman's apparent death notice arrived in April 1973. National Life Chairman William C. Weaver, Jr., had commissioned a study by New York theatre design authority Jo Mielziner. His assessment was bleak.

"It would be unprofessional for me as a theatrical designer…to recommend the preservation or the reconstruction of the Ryman," he wrote. "It would be far less expensive to build a modern concert hall and a legitimate theatre than to take down and redesign within the stringent limitations of this 1891 structure." After two days of inspection, Mielziner found fault with the structure's original construction, its prospects for dressing room or rest room space, its sight lines, and a host of other shortcomings. All he could recommend salvaging were the building's pews, some carved stone, the balcony's Confederate Gallery sign, and "possibly some of the cast iron columns now partly supporting the gallery."

As if to head off criticism, Mielziner noted that he had come to Nashville in part at the recommendation of Benjamin H. Caldwell, president of the Tennessee Historic Sites Federation, whom he said "valued his judgment and would rely on it." However, Caldwell immediately shot back that the report was "incomplete" and "superficial."

"I respect Mr. Mielziner's ability as a theatre and stage designer and there is no doubt that the conclusion he reached concerning the inadequacies of the Ryman Auditorium are correct," Caldwell said. "But he is neither a historian nor an architect. When he comments on these areas, he is speaking beyond his realm of knowledge."

Local preservationist groups had weighed in on behalf of saving the building even before the report was issued, and the document gave them a rallying point. Tennessee's U.S. Senators Howard Baker and Bill Brock intervened, urging National Life to preserve the building. They pressed the Nixon White House into sending a two-person delegation to Nashville to tour the Ryman and express—albeit vaguely— the president's "interest" in the building.

Washington-based historian Thomas Merrick Slade from the National Trust for Historic Preservation weighed in on behalf of saving the building "at any cost." Another major endorsement came from *The New York Times* architecture critic Ada Louise Huxtable. In her Sunday column, she lacerated National Life's opposition to saving the structure as "a mixture of architectural ignorance and astute business venality." She noted that razing the Ryman would mean "abandonment of a neighborhood that needs help, and speeding the death of downtown." Good urban design, she wrote, would use the Ryman as a centerpiece of downtown redevelopment. As for the Little Church of Opryland, she offered "first prize for the pious misuse of a landmark."

Huxtable's column invigorated preservation activists, who organized public hearings and letters to the editor campaigns. Gradually, National Life's position shifted. All options were open, they said; the wrecking ball was not going to swing the week after the Opry left the building.

The auditorium was structurally sound but far from ready to host concerts. It was painted industrial gray inside and had no decent bathrooms. The box office on the Fifth Avenue side was a picture of dilapidated inefficiency, but National Life was in no position to commit to a full revitalization. Yet it seemed wrong to keep the faithful and the curious out or to keep the building in mothballs. So, about a week before the last Opry performance, Ryman officials announced that they would open up the building for tours.

For only a dollar visitors could walk into the resonant room and study it like a decommissioned battleship. National Life bundled the Ryman in its bus tour of Nashville, attracting

Sissy Spacek stars as Loretta Lynn along with the real Minnie Pearl and Ernest Tubb in Coal Miner's Daughter.

Grand Ole Opry Archives

about 1,400 people a month to the building. Another 600 dropped in on their own to sit in the pews, talk with tour guides, view a rudimentary museum of the Ryman's past, and stand before a microphone on the former Opry stage.

Few events were organized in the hall during the deserted 1970s and 1980s, but the Ryman did become a popular set for filmmakers. In 1975, Burt Reynolds starred in *W.W. and the Dixie Dancekings* as a conman and thief who delivers on his promise to get a struggling country band (including musicians portrayed by Jerry Reed and Don Williams) a spot on the Grand Ole Opry. *Elvis,* a 1979 ABC television movie directed by John Carpenter, starred Kurt Russell as Elvis Presley in a stellar albeit historically inaccurate reenactment of his 1954 Opry appearance. *Coal Miner's Daughter* (1980), the Oscar-winning film about Loretta Lynn's life and career, and *Sweet*

Dreams (1985), the Patsy Cline biopic, were filmed inside and outside of the Ryman, recreating events in both of the women's lives where they actually happened. Clint Eastwood performed his own vocals and guitar work for *Honkytonk Man* (1982), which follows an ailing country singer as he takes his final shot at the big time and auditions for the Grand Ole Opry.

In 1983, the Ryman changed corporate ownership when National Life's new parent company, American General Life Insurance Company of Dallas, sold the building, along with WSM radio, Opryland Hotel, the Grand Ole Opry, and Opryland USA to Gaylord Broadcasting Company of Oklahoma City. Six years later, Gaylord invested a million dollars in the hall's exterior. The facelift included a new roof, mortar, gutters, and windows. *The Tennessean* editorialized that with the Ryman in the vanguard, downtown "is coming back as the city's hub."

Ever so slowly, downtown began to change just outside the Ryman's doors. Merchant's, which was originally opened the same year as the Ryman, and now stands as a restaurant on Fourth and Broadway, was a harbinger of fashionable night-life on Lower Broadway. The Nashville Convention Center, completed in 1987, bordered the Ryman on its Fifth Avenue side with a sleek new edifice. In 1991, on another side of the Ryman, work began on the AT&T tower, the tallest building in Tennessee. By the mid-1990s, the Ryman's Gothic Revival structure sat next to these aged and modern monoliths, lending a comfortable old-meets-new flavor to the city's core.

While Gaylord Entertainment deliberated plans for the Ryman's interior and future use, several events took place on its stage that sent clear signals that music still had a home there. In 1988, superstar Dolly Parton assembled a reunion of female country legends, including Kitty Wells, Jean Shepard, Minnie Pearl, and Jan Howard, at the Ryman for an episode of her ABC variety show. The year 1991 was a pivotal year for the Mother Church. In April, The Nashville Network (TNN) used the Ryman as the location for a series of country music television shows before small audiences of about 250 spectators. In May, eclectic country songbird Emmylou Harris borrowed

Gaylord Entertainment Company's 1989 exterior renovation and stabilization project included the restoration of Ryman Auditorium's 144 windows to glass.

Donnie Beauchamp photograph, Grand Ole Opry Archives

the stage to record a live album called *At the Ryman* with her band, the Nash Ramblers. Perhaps more than any other event, this concert, which included a guest appearance by bluegrass founding father Bill Monroe, foreshadowed the Ryman's return as a great showplace.

During the taping of her ABC variety show in 1988, Dolly Parton reminisced at the Ryman with (left to right) Kitty Wells, Del Wood, Jan Howard, Skeeter Davis, Minnie Pearl, Jeanne Pruett, Norma Jean, and Jean Shepard. Looking on is country music booking agent, Billy Deaton.

Donnie Beauchamp photograph, Grand Ole Opry Archives

In May 1992, Gaylord Entertainment hosted a centennial celebration for the Ryman that offered plenty of vivid reminders of what the Ryman had been like in its final Grand Ole Opry years. It was uncomfortably hot. The pews had splinters, pink insulation poked through cracks in the ceiling, and the balcony was deemed too decrepit to seat anyone safely. Despite the discomfort, however, stars such as Connie Smith, Vince Gill, Ricky Skaggs, Bill Monroe, and others put on an entertaining and moving show for a crowd of about 700. After careful deliberation, Monroe decided he and his band should not wear their hats to perform gospel music in what he knew had originally been a church. WTVF-Channel 5 news anchor, Bud Hedinger, told the building's story—of Tom Ryman, Sam Jones, and the promised grand tabernacle—in dramatic form, breathing life into the origins of the hall for a new generation of city leaders.

Finally, in October 1992, inspired in large part by the centenary celebration's success and the passion of the artists who had recently performed at the Ryman, Gaylord announced the auditorium's full-fledged renaissance. Chairman E.W. "Bud" Wendell held a press conference, saying, "We're committed to a renovation of the Ryman as quick as we can get it done." Plans called for an $8.5 million restoration and a projected reopening in early 1994. A new, architecturally complementary annex would house the Ryman offices, restrooms, box office, concessions, and gift shop. The new structure would also hold critical systems such as fire control and the answer to the prayers of patron and performers alike: central heat and air conditioning. The plan also included a more complete and refined museum, with cases of Ryman memorabilia nested comfortably in the back of the hall itself and in the old Fifth Avenue vestibule. Most important was Wendell's promise that the new Ryman would be "one of America's coveted performance locations."

The new annex reoriented the Ryman's public face. The hall's front door is now on Fourth Avenue, while its grand Fifth Avenue façade is now a decorative edifice photographed so often that it has become as iconic for Nashville as the statue of Liberty is for New York City. Outside the new entrance is a small plaza with a view of Nashville's tallest skyscraper, the twin-spire AT&T Building—affectionately known as the "Batman building"—across the street. The enormous Tennessee poplar sliding pocket doors that once greeted visitors entering from the Fifth Avenue side did not meet modern fire and evacuation standards, so they were restored to pristine condition and displayed inside the main floor entrance to the auditorium as a symbol of renewal.

The auditorium itself did not need radical remodeling. Officials were pleased to find that the balcony was structurally solid after all, with only segments of the floor rotted from soft drink syrup where the concession areas had been. The orchestra level floor immediately in front of the stage also

On what had been the back side of the Ryman, an addition was constructed for offices, restrooms, concessions, a gift shop, and ticket office. The entrance moved from Fifth to Fourth Avenue.

Donnie Beauchamp photograph, Grand Ole Opry Archives

needed replacing. After the pews were removed, it proved sufficient to clean and revarnish the rest of the old tongue-in-groove pine floors. On the ceiling, the situation was much the same; the odd board needed replacing or mending, but the resonant surface remained essentially the same as it was in 1892.

The concentric, curved pews, one of the Ryman's most precious assets and distinctive features, needed special attention. Two hundred and fifty individual lengths totaling 4,000 feet of seat space were removed and trucked to Leeds, Alabama. The Leeds Seating Company scraped them clean of many pounds of gum, sanded them where necessary, varnished them, and left years of nicks and knocks just as they were.

Within the auditorium, every effort was made to refurbish, restore, or repair as many of the original elements as possible. The result is an exceptionally authentic space that allows visitors to sense the building's historic nature the moment they enter the 1892 structure. Backstage areas needed

In the most visible change to the original auditorium, sections of the balcony were removed on each side of the stage. Structures were then erected on each side to house dressing rooms, an elevator, a production office, and a catering room.

Donnie Beauchamp photograph, Grand Ole Opry Archives

the most serious reconstruction. With only a huge curtain separating the audience from the stage apparatus, there had never been a proscenium save for a temporary wall erected during the later Opry years. The Confederate Gallery balcony still extended around the stage to the back walls of the Ryman just as it had when it was built in 1897. Modifications included a metal frame and drywall proscenium erected across the theatre a few feet back from the front of the stage. Behind that, as construction director Walker Mathews described it in a newspaper article, the equivalent of a pair of four-story buildings was erected on both flanks of the stage. Here at last the old hall could have dressing rooms fit for stars and bands and theatre troupes, with "amenities" like plumbing, an elevator, and a catering room. The hidden towers also became home for amplification and recording systems.

Because only black and white photographs of the Ryman were available from its early days, contractors

The stage in the renovated auditorium, dating from 1951, was preserved and framed by a new proscenium wall. State of the art lighting and sound systems prepared the venue for modern productions, both live and recorded.

Donnie Beauchamp photograph, Grand Ole Opry Archives

researched the auditorium's original colors by scraping through layers of paint. They found not only a soft green palette for the walls, but a painted decorative pattern on the Confederate Gallery that they re-created for the newly plastered balcony.

Workmen dug trenches under the building for heat and air conditioning ducts and removed four enormous fans that had been the room's only cooling system for decades. They also removed big steam radiators in front of the stage and footlights on the stage. In the cavernous attic, they built an elaborate lighting elevation system with winches and cables that poked through the ceiling to suspended light rails. When they removed a wall in the Fifth Avenue vestibule they discovered one of the Ryman's original toilets—a commode over a pit— little more than an indoor privy.

New lighting was either unobtrusive or designed to reflect the Ryman's period architecture. The original gas lamps that had hung from the ceiling were recreated in electric versions to hang beneath the balcony where their scale was more appropriate, and custom turn-of-the-century-style chandeliers were hung from the ceiling and supplemented with recessed pin lights.

The new lobby received much scrutiny because it would welcome audiences and offer an important transitional space between the street and the hallowed hall, as well as a connection between the present and past. Before the lobby annex was built, the space "behind" the Ryman was a gravel parking lot for buses, with two large arched doors at ground level and a row of Gothic windows above. Architects Hart-Freeland-Roberts built the annex to span both floors, turning the original upstairs windows into doors and the lower doors into the natural arch of a theatre entrance. A symmetrical staircase in the lobby was decorated with iron patterns replicated from period stairwells within the Ryman proper. The exterior of the addition features a modernized version of the Ryman's Gothic architecture with arched windows and red brick façade, but it remains distinct from the original building.

With its furnishings updated and its pews back in place, the Ryman was ready to be a theatre again. Its inaugural event however was a private one: the wedding of country star Trisha Yearwood and Mavericks bass player Robert Reynolds in May of 1994. Mavericks front man Raul Malo and the Del McCoury Band performed for about 400 guests.

Shortly after that, the Ryman hosted a CBS television special, co-produced by the legendary Quincy Jones, titled "The Roots of Country: Nashville Celebrates the Ryman." The house sound system barely was finished in time, and the television crew got into trouble for moving some of the Ryman's newly restored pews, but big exterior floodlights gave the stained glass windows a warm, welcoming glow inside. Charismatic country artist Marty Stuart, the night's musical director, led a remarkable array of artists in paying tribute to the room's storied past and pointing it toward a bright future.

The cast included Earl Scruggs, Carl Perkins, Chet Atkins, Johnny Cash, Vince Gill, Alan Jackson, Hal Ketchum, Alison Krauss, Patty Loveless, Kathy Mattea, Reba McEntire,

Among the guests featured on the first broadcast of A Prairie Home Companion *from the Ryman were Vince Gill, Mary Chapin Carpenter, and the Everly Brothers.*

Donnie Beauchamp photograph, Grand Ole Opry Archives

Lee Roy Parnell, Pam Tillis, Steve Wariner, and Sam Moore from the soul duo Sam and Dave. The artists each contributed to a time capsule, a five-foot high safe carried with great effort down a set of narrow stairs and placed under the stage. Its plaque stipulates that it will be opened on or after June 1, 2044. Stuart summed up the night to *The Washington Post*: "I looked down off the stage, and to my left there was Quincy Jones and Nastassja Kinski. I saw Bill Monroe, Kitty Wells, Loretta Lynn, the Mavericks. I saw a lot of bluegrass musicians and new country musicians and gospel singers. The Ryman is the mother church of country music. And what does a church house do? It opens its arms and welcomes all."

On the night of June 4, 1994, the curtain officially went up on the restored Ryman. Garrison Keillor hosted a gala grand opening show. The live broadcast of *A Prairie Home Companion* featured Chet Atkins, the Everly Brothers, Robin and Linda Williams, Mary Chapin Carpenter, Mark O'Connor, and Vince Gill. Keillor related how, twenty years prior, he had been inspired to launch his popular public radio show while in Nashville writing a New Yorker article about the Grand Ole Opry's last show in the Ryman. In the folksy cadence familiar to millions of public radio listeners, Keillor reminisced about that visit, including the curious onlookers who could not get in but who watched through the Ryman's half-opened ground-floor windows: "You couldn't see anybody who stood over about 5 feet, 4 inches, so you couldn't see Porter Wagoner's hair, but you could see all of Little Jimmy Dickens and the important parts of Dolly Parton," he avowed.

© 1996 Hatch Show Print

VI. Ryman Auditorium Today

When the refurbished Ryman threw open its doors in 1994, it was poised to reclaim its place as Nashville's premiere performance venue. In looking to the future, the Ryman embraced its glorious past, once again realizing its original mission: to be a place where all are welcome.

In the years following the reopening, the building expanded its reputation for variety by hosting prominent artists from across the musical spectrum. Among the many standout shows in the first five years were performances by legends Bob Dylan, the Everly Brothers, and James Brown; contemporary hit makers Beck, Dave Mathews, Lenny Kravitz, and Sheryl Crow; jazz masters Chick Corea, Harry Connick, Jr., and Wynton Marsalis; country legends George Jones, Merle Haggard, and Waylon Jennings; folk father figure Doc Watson; and bluesman Robert Cray. The eclectic and noteworthy programming helped transform the Ryman's image from a venerated vessel of vaudeville and country music's golden era to a cutting-edge concert venue among the finest in the nation.

In December 1996, rock icon Bruce Springsteen validated the stature of the hall in the early post-renovation years. The Grammy-winning working class hero had not played Nashville since 1984's full-tilt "Born in the U.S.A." tour with the world-famous E Street Band, and Ryman general manager Steve Buchanan had Springsteen high on his wish list. Buchanan credits Emmylou Harris for the connection, because she told Springsteen at a joint appearance in New York City about the Ryman's special vibe and urged him to book a show. Springsteen's reputation as an arena rocker is known worldwide, but among songwriters in a songwriter's town like Nashville, he is as revered as Bob Dylan, Paul Simon, or Kris Kristofferson. For nearly three hours, Springsteen performed solo with an acoustic guitar, focusing on songs he'd written for the recently released *The Ghost of Tom Joad,* a concept album inspired by John Steinbeck's novel *The Grapes of Wrath.*

Springsteen told the audience, "It's an honor for me to be on this stage and in this building," and tied the Ryman's magic to his love for country music. "Country," he said, "wasn't afraid to ask hard questions about adult life, and it wasn't satisfied with escapist, easy answers." *The Tennessean's* Tom Roland wrote that "Springsteen gave [the audience] a concert with a local feel. He created the kind of songwriter guitar-pull [informal playing sessions] that one witnesses at small clubs and in musicians' homes."

No sooner did performers begin playing the old hall than they began singing its praises before, during, and after their shows. Anticipating a September 1994 date, singer-songwriter Rodney Crowell told *The Tennessean,* "I think my reverence is gonna really kick in.… I'm very respectful of history and music. I'm a student in that way, so it's not lost on me that we're all gonna get to play the Ryman." In late 1995, following a TNN television taping, Vince Gill told *USA Today* that the Ryman was the "most amazing place I've ever sung in. The acoustics, the way the music reverberates and decays, is so perfect. It dies without all those odd overtones that big arenas have. The first time I sang in there, the heat went all through my body when I started singing. It was definitely a spiritual vibe, an awesome feeling." Artist guest books began filling up with hand-written remarks that ranged from the humbled and inspired to the mystical. Bob Dylan nodded to "the Boys and ghosts of the Old Brigade (like a fleet of Wild Horses Passing)." Kris Kristofferson thanked the Ryman for "a very spiritual experience." And Trisha Yearwood wrote "I've had this dream from a tender age/Callin' my name from the Opry Stage," a couplet from her song "Wrong Side of Memphis." In 2003, country legend George Jones wrote, "What an honor. I'm living my dream tonight." Amy Grant shared, "I have dreamed of

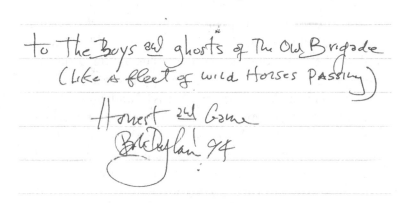

To the Boys and ghosts of The Old Brigade
(like a fleet of wild Horses passing)

Honest and Game
Bob Dylan '94

Bob Dylan's enigmatic guest book entry
Ryman Auditorium Collection

singing on this stage. How wonderful to be a part of a place that
honors not only where we are going—who we are becoming—
but celebrates where we have been & all that we come from.
Sing on." Earl Scruggs, who met his beloved wife Louise at the
Ryman, wrote in 1994, "It's good to come back to the Ryman
again. Sure brings back good memories." John Paul White of
The Civil Wars wrote "…dreamed of this day. It was better than
a dream."

Artists from all genres relished their time in the
refurbished Ryman Auditorium. A classical music series, which
brought in the Academy of St. Martin-in-the-Fields, the Julliard
String Quartet, and the Vienna Boys Choir, among others,
called forth memories of early twentieth-century performances
by the likes of the New York Philharmonic. The Chieftains
hinted at the worldly roots music that would be common on
the Ryman stage in coming years by playing their renowned
traditional Irish repertoire. The Boys Choir of Harlem and
The Tennessee Dance Theatre performed, and the Nashville
Symphony paired its classical orchestration with country
singers like Lorrie Morgan.

Sam's Place: Music for the Spirit was a Sunday night Christian music series named for Sam Jones and hosted by artist and hit songwriter Gary Chapman. The show called upon the skills of a wide array of gospel and contemporary Christian music stars, including DC Talk, the Fairfield Four, the Gaither Vocal Band, Vestal Goodman, and Jerry and Tammy Sullivan. Particularly resonant were the cherished spirituals of the Fisk Jubilee Singers, the world-famous chorus of undergraduates from Nashville's Fisk University that had been a part of Ryman history since 1892. *Sam's Place* also made a commitment to feature the connection between gospel and country music, with guest appearances by country stars like Bill Monroe, Wynonna, Charlie Daniels, Faith Hill, and Alison Krauss.

Soon after reopening, the Ryman also resumed its role as an important venue for civic events. Benefit concerts on behalf of a wide range of regional and national nonprofit organizations have taken the stage, raising funds and awareness for critical health and societal issues. In August 1996, political affairs returned to the auditorium with a 48th birthday party for Tipper Gore, during which 1,900 guests raised money for the Tennessee Democratic Party. Emceed by K.T. Oslin and BeBe Winans, the evening also featured performances by Sawyer Brown, the Fairfield Four, and John Hiatt as well as a live satellite appearance by then-president Bill Clinton, who was simultaneously celebrating his birthday in New York.

In October 2008, when the internationally televised presidential debate between Senators Barack Obama and John McCain came to the nearby Belmont University campus, the Ryman was a key companion venue. On the Sunday night prior to the debate, a special edition of the Opry was staged for the political community and international media attending the historic event. It featured Belmont alumni Josh Turner, Brad Paisley, Julie Roberts, and Trisha Yearwood, plus a surprise singing appearance by CBS news veteran and country music fan Bob Schieffer. The seasoned broadcaster admitted to feeling nervous about his Opry debut—more so than about the televised presidential debate he was scheduled to moderate the following weekend. Schieffer commented, "After you've stood on that Opry stage, nothing really scares you and for sure, nothing could be more fun." On October 7, the debate itself was simulcast inside the Ryman for the many VIP guests who could not be accommodated at the Belmont debate hall.

As the Country Music Association first did in 1968 for the CMA Awards, many music organizations have chosen Ryman Auditorium to host their honors and awards programs. The Academy of Country Music (ACM); the Americana Music Association (AMA); the American Society of Composers, Authors, and Publishers (ASCAP); the International Bluegrass Music Association (IBMA); the International Entertainment Buyers Association (IEBA); the National Academy of Recording Arts and Sciences (NARAS); and concert and touring industry association Pollstar have all honored their best and brightest at the Ryman.

Bluegrass music was born on the Ryman stage and retains an indelible connection to the building. In celebration of the shared musical heritage, a bluegrass series was inaugurated not long after the 1994 reopening. The series offered a lineup featuring the top artists at work in the genre. By opening with a double bill of bluegrass originator Monroe himself, and then-newcomer Alison Krauss, the series celebrated both the music's pioneers and modern-day risk takers. The rest of that year's lineup included Marty Stuart, the Osborne Brothers, John Hartford, and other era-shaping artists. The summer series continues to showcase the best in bluegrass—from traditionalists like Ralph Stanley, Ricky Skaggs, and The Del McCoury Band to the more off-beat artists of the genre such as Sam Bush, Dailey & Vincent, Old Crow Medicine Show, and Chris Thile. Country music superstar Vince Gill has frequently assembled an A-list bluegrass ensemble for the series.

In the fall of 2006, during the IBMA's annual convention, the Tennessee Historical Commission presented the Ryman with a historical marker commemorating it as the birthplace of bluegrass. Earl Scruggs was on hand, along with other bluegrass royalty, to dedicate the new marker at the northwest corner of the building. Modern-day master Ricky Skaggs, a protégé of Monroe, said to the assembled crowd on

Bluegrass pioneer Earl Scruggs inspects the historic marker com-memorating the Ryman as the birthplace of bluegrass music.

The Tennessean

a beautiful September afternoon that "lovers of bluegrass have always known that WSM, the air castle of the South, was really the first blast of this music out to the airwaves from right here at the Grand Ole Opry."

The renovated Ryman also returned to its theatrical roots, and its modern-day forays into theatre have been successful—even triumphant. Although *Always...Patsy Cline* did not premiere at the Ryman, it would, on the strength of 19-year-old Tennessee native Mandy Barnett in the title role, be forever associated with the Mother Church even as it toured the nation. The two-act, two-woman musical created by Ted Swindley documents the relationship between Cline and fan Louise Seger. Swindley would say that opening the show's extended run at the Ryman in the mid-1990s, where some 200,000 people saw the show, was "probably more important than playing Broadway."

Not long thereafter, another musical based on the life of a country legend opened at the Ryman. *Lost Highway: The Music and Legend of Hank Williams* featured Jason Petty,

Mandy Barnett stars as the great Patsy Cline with Tere Myers as fan Louise Seger in the 2011 production of Always...Patsy Cline.

Steve Lowry photograph, Ryman Auditorium Archives

who was discovered impersonating Williams at Opryland. After successful runs in 1996 and 1997, the show eventually moved to New York, where it became one of the best-received Nashville-born shows in history, playing off-Broadway to rave reviews. Petty was nominated for a Drama Desk Award for his portrayal of the incomparable artist Williams.

Lost Highway and *Always...Patsy Cline* had been produced by independent companies and staged at the Ryman, but two subsequent musicals were launched and overseen by the Ryman's organization. *Bye Bye Love: the Everly Brothers Musical,* launched in 1998, was a theatrical biography of the rock icons who were discovered at the Ryman's back entrance and rose to fame on the Opry. Three years later, the Ryman premiered a musical stage show recounting the life and music of the brilliant but star-crossed Tammy Wynette. *Stand By Your Man* featured episodes that had originally occurred at the Ryman, including the production's finale of Wynette's memorial service. The series of musicals celebrating iconic country stars, all of whom had performed at the Ryman as members of the

Opry cast, resurrected two of the Ryman's most important past lives in an unexpected and inspired way. Certainly Lula Naff would have been bemused by the development.

Finally, time was squarely on the Ryman's side. It had made a tremendous comeback and was now securely reestablished as a vital performance venue. The structure itself is a significant Nashville architectural artifact. It has been on the National Register of Historic Places since 1971, and in June 2001 was awarded National Historic Landmark status, a superlative honor.

Given its celebrated past and vibrant present, it is not surprising that a diverse array of visitors from across the globe is interested in learning more about the Ryman in person— more than three million in the first two decades following the reopening. History buffs, architecture aficionados, Opry devotees, and fans of all genres of music and live entertainment flock to the Ryman for daytime tours. In the auditorium, guests encounter artifacts from Tom Ryman's home and career, memorabilia from Lula Naff's tenure as the theatre's in-house impresario, stage costumes worn by Opry stars, and instruments played by legendary artists. Audio visual displays feature historical performances from the legendary stage and artists telling their own Ryman stories. In the Ryman Recording Studio, visitors can record their own version of hit songs by artists like Garth Brooks, Patsy Cline, and Taylor Swift while looking at the very stage where the original singers performed to enthusiastic crowds. They can join guided backstage tours and visit the historically-themed dressing rooms used by contemporary artists while hearing stories of the Ryman's early days. Photographs, programs, and advertisements illustrating many of the luminaries from the fields of music, opera, theatre, dance, education, religion, and politics who have appeared in the hall, paint a rich picture of the Ryman's diverse history in a 75-foot graphic timeline that is located in the second floor Fifth Avenue vestibule.

Through the years, the Ryman's temporary exhibits have displayed artifacts and highlighted important personalities from its past, including Johnny Cash and June Carter, Minnie

Pearl, and Patsy Cline. The exhibit "Ryman Stage to Screen" was inspired by the movies and TV shows shot on location over the years—another important chapter in the Ryman story.

The Ryman's outstanding acoustics are widely revered, but with its warm wood tones, stained glass windows, curved balcony, and open and airy yet intimate interior space, the auditorium is also visually stunning. This combination of superior sight and sound has attracted many film and television productions since the reopening. One of the first television specials to come to the Ryman was Neil Diamond's "Under a Tennessee Moon," which aired on ABC in 1996. A companion piece to Diamond's gold-selling record, *Tennessee Moon*, it paired the iconic artist and songwriter with his Nashville collaborators featured on the album, including Chet Atkins, Waylon Jennings, and Beth Nielsen Chapman, and co-writers Harlan Howard, Richard Bennett, and Gary Nicholson.

In May of 2000, a clutch of bluegrass, gospel, and old-time country artists performed music from an upcoming film by brothers Joel and Ethan Coen titled *O Brother, Where Art Thou?* Before the film was released, producer and music supervisor T-Bone Burnett and others arranged a concert at the Ryman to showcase the soundtrack and contributing musicians. Renowned music documentarian D.A. Pennebaker was on hand to capture the event, titled *Down from the Mountain.* Gospel greats the Fairfield Four, Opry veterans the Whites, mountain-singing legend Ralph Stanley, nouveau old-time duo Gillian Welch and David Rawlings, and guitar picking wonder Norman Blake were among the cast. The emcee was fiddler/songwriter/raconteur John Hartford, one of Nashville's most beloved figures.

Willie Nelson produced some quintessential Ryman moments as he approached his 70th birthday. For an April 2002 USA Network taping, he assembled one of the most varied lineups ever to play the hall. He sang the Rolling Stones classic "Dead Flowers," backed by Stones guitar hero Keith Richards, Hank Williams III (grandson of the country icon), and songwriter Ryan Adams. Nelson's recent duet partners Sheryl Crow, Norah Jones, and R&B crooner Brian McKnight also

Gospel group the Fairfield Four kicks off the Down from the Mountain concert with the traditional work song, "Po' Lazarus."

© Beth Gwinn, courtesy Universal Music Group

shared the stage, as did Country Music Hall of Fame member Ray Price, the Dixie Chicks, Toby Keith, Matchbox Twenty vocalist Rob Thomas, and rockers Jon Bon Jovi and Richie Sambora. When Vince Gill sang the Buffalo Springfield classic, "For What It's Worth," the line, "There's something happening here. What it is ain't exactly clear," proved particularly fitting.

Vince Gill chose the Ryman as the venue for his HDNet television special, which highlighted just how perfect the hall looked in the new medium of high definition television. A year later in 2008, Alan Jackson was honored during a taping of *CMT Giants* by special guests, including Hank Williams, Jr., Miranda Lambert, Martina McBride, Brad Paisley, George Strait, Taylor Swift, and Lee Ann Womack. Other notable full-length concert videos taped at the Ryman include *Norah Jones and the Handsome Band: Live in 2004*, Foreigner's *Rockin' at the Ryman* (2010), *Levon Helm's Ramble at the Ryman* (2011), *The Raconteurs Live at the Ryman Auditorium 9.5.11*, and Ringo Starr's *Ringo at the Ryman* (2013).

Television series have been drawn to the Ryman, including *American Idol*, which held auditions for its 2011 season in the hall. Making the grade with *Idol* judges Randy Jackson, Steven Tyler, and Jennifer Lopez was country artist Lauren Alaina, who not only went on to Hollywood, but was runner-up for the season, propelling her to a record deal and performances on the Grand Ole Opry.

The ABC musical drama *Nashville,* which showcases Nashville's music scene and signature places, has used the Ryman as a location several times, including an entire episode of the first season based around a concert at the Ryman. The episode features characters Rayna Jaymes (Connie Britton) and Juliette Barnes (Hayden Panettiere) as they set aside their differences and introduce a new duet from the Ryman stage. The premise for the performance is a showcase for their record label that is not unlike real showcases that have taken place at the Ryman.

Music videos are another medium that have enlisted the Ryman as a co-star. Videos for Gretchen Wilson's "When I Think About Cheating," Kellie Pickler's "I Wonder," Darius Rucker's, "This," Alan Jackson's "Precious Memories," and Lee Brice's "I Don't Dance," each have a very different tone, demonstrating that the Ryman has the ability to reflect a great range of emotion.

Perhaps no filmed event at the renovated Ryman exceeded the stature of Neil Young's ambitious *Heart of Gold.* In August 2005, filmmaker Jonathan Demme (*Stop Making Sense, Silence of the Lambs*) directed Young, his band, and distinguished musical guests such as Emmylou Harris, Spooner Oldham, and the Fisk Jubilee Singers to perform Young's new album *A Prairie Wind* in its entirety along with Young's standards such as "Heart of Gold" and "Old Man." The concert film was released nationwide to great critical acclaim. Carrie Rickey of the *Philadelphia Inquirer* put it simply, "It's movie and music bliss." Said Young about the experience and the hall, "It's like…Mecca. There's anticipation, but not fear. It's rewarding. It rewards you. It is one of, if not the best, sounding halls that I've ever played in. It's like country music heaven."

Country music heaven, indeed. Even as the Ryman showcased a diversity of entertainment that had not been seen on its stage since the 1950s, its identity as the "Mother Church of Country Music," remained as strong as ever. From Alabama to Zac Brown Band, country artists have relished the opportunity to play the historic venue and often choose the Ryman to host important career moments.

Miranda Lambert, contemporary purveyor of country music's outlaw attitude, showed a soft spot for the Mother Church when she kissed the stage during "Revolution at the Ryman," an exclusive concert at which she debuted her 2009 platinum-selling album, *Revolution.* An unexpected debut took place in 2012 on the night that country queen Loretta Lynn interrupted a performance of the *Opry Country Classics* show to welcome singer/songwriter/actress Zooey Deschanel to the stage and to reveal that a Broadway musical version of Lynn's autobiography, *Coal Miner's Daughter,* would be developed with Deschanel in the lead. The two then treated the audience to a duet of the title song. The significance of such events is underscored when they unfold on the stage of the Ryman.

For many country artists, there is no bigger career milestone than performing for the Mother Church's original country congregation at the Opry. It had seemed inevitable since the Ryman's reopening in 1994 that the Grand Ole Opry would return to its former home, but it did not happen until the winter of 1999. Steve Buchanan, then general manager of the Grand Ole Opry, said Gaylord officials were hesitant to send the show back to its most storied stage too early in the Ryman's comeback, preferring to give the hall a chance to develop a solid identity of its own.

"We wanted to truly reflect the Ryman's heritage, which was far more extensive than just having been the home of the Grand Ole Opry," Buchanan said. "We sensed it was really important to create a separation, because the Ryman, to many, was still the Opry House. But with time, the Ryman's unique and diverse identity took hold and then the time was right to bring the Opry back down and recreate that connection."

So, a quarter century after the Opry's move to Opryland, excitement over how the show would look and sound in the refurbished hall was palpable. Before the curtain rose on January 15 and 16, 1999, there were bluegrass jams in the acoustically lively stairwells and elbow-to-elbow visiting backstage among the artists and musicians, just like old times.

With a signature barn backdrop and an excited audience out front, a range of artists who remembered years of Opry shows in the old hall were on hand to perform, including Porter Wagoner, Little Jimmy Dickens, Bill Carlisle, and Jeanne Pruett. Del McCoury, a one-time member of Bill Monroe's Blue Grass Boys, performed with his sons, along with country stars Vince Gill, Joe Diffie, and Martina McBride. As the climax of the first weekend back, Trisha Yearwood was surprised with an invitation to join the Opry.

"This has the feeling of winning Female Vocalist of the Year, something I wanted my whole life," Yearwood told CMT. "For my family, especially my parents, this is probably bigger than any award I've received. My mom once saw the Opry here at the Ryman. She wrote down descriptions of the Opry stars and the show, so she could take it home and show her mom and dad. She still has that diary, and it was really neat for me to see what it had meant to her. I feel proud…."

The potent, nostalgic combination of the Ryman building and the Grand Ole Opry broadcast was such a success that the Opry now has a tradition of spending the winter months at the Ryman. The shows have a warmth and intimacy that visitors and artists cherish, and Ryman-based Opry inductions have taken on a special significance as well. One of the first to be so honored was modern-day traditionalist Brad Paisley in the winter of 2001. For the occasion he borrowed a special piece of costuming from his friend Buck Owens—an embroidered yellow jacket designed by the famous country music tailor Nudie Cohn and worn by Owens on the cover of his 1966 *Carnegie Hall Concert* album. Paisley was also the first new member to receive the Opry Member Award, a 14-inch bronze and oak trophy cast in the form of the iconic Grand Ole Opry microphone stand on a base made of wood from

Brad Paisley clutches his Opry Member Award as he is welcomed into the Opry cast by fellow member, Steve Wariner, on February 17, 2001.

Randy Piland photograph, Grand Ole Opry Archives

the Ryman pews that came available during renovation. The creation of the award marked the seventy-fifth anniversary of the world's longest-running radio show as well as the return of the Opry to its most famous historic venue. Although the Opry has now been at the Grand Ole Opry House longer than any of its other homes, including the Ryman, the special bond between Tom Ryman's tabernacle and country music's proudest tradition is perennial.

That bond may be most powerful when the hall is called upon as a location for funerals, as it was for bluegrass groundbreaker Bill Monroe. On September 11, 1996, Monroe lied in state amid gardens of flowers in front of the stage where in the late 1940s he had fused old-time string band music with swing and pre-rock 'n' roll swagger. Stacks of quarters, his customary gift to admiring children, lined the edge of the casket. After chilling yet comforting performances of traditional sacred songs like "Wayfaring Stranger" and "How

Great Thou Art," Ricky Skaggs and Marty Stuart led a band through the salty, secular Monroe mandolin instrumental "Rawhide" for an audience of some 1,500 people. Bagpipers playing "Amazing Grace" escorted the casket out of the Mother Church.

Sixteen years later, the Ryman would host a funeral of another forefather of bluegrass: Earl Scruggs. During the service on a warm April afternoon in 2012, artists such as Del McCoury, Ricky Skaggs, Bela Fleck, Emmylou Harris, Vince Gill, John McEuen, and Marty Stuart paid homage to the man who is credited with helping to create modern country music with his trailblazing style of banjo playing.

Through the years, the hall has hosted funerals or memorial services for a range of iconic artists and business figures, including producer and Music Row pioneer Owen Bradley; "Nashville Sound" innovator and guitar wizard Chet Atkins; crossover superstar Eddy Arnold; classic Nashville songwriter Harlan Howard; outlaw legend Waylon Jennings; Opry legends Skeeter Davis, Jack Greene, and Jimmy C. Newman; and industry veteran and producer Buddy Killen. In each case, the public joined the friends, family, and music industry figures who turned out to speak, sing, or just sit and listen to testimony about lives and careers that have animated Music City's spirit.

The memorial for Johnny Cash was especially momentous. Cash passed away at age seventy-one, leaving a magnificent legacy and a void in American culture. His wife and constant companion, June Carter Cash, had passed away a mere four months earlier. Although the funeral for The Man in Black was private, some weeks later the Cash family organized a memorial concert. The ideal location was obvious. Cash debuted at the Ryman on the Grand Ole Opry in 1956, and it was backstage that year that he approached June Carter of the famous Carter Family and introduced himself. *The Johnny Cash Show* further cemented the affiliation.

On November 9, 2003, Cash's brother Tommy welcomed a packed house of fans from as far away as the Czech Republic to pay tribute to "the greatest man I ever knew." An

extraordinary parade of artists, most with personal connections to Cash, performed equally personal versions of Cash songs.

Daughter Rosanne offered a plaintive rendition of "I Still Miss Someone." Stepdaughter Carlene Carter and country star Ronnie Dunn, who was wearing a black coat Cash had given him when Dunn was a Nashville newcomer, performed an uproarious duet of "Jackson." And at one point Willie Nelson, Kris Kristofferson, George Jones, and Hank Williams, Jr., were on stage together—the giants of country music's outlaw era paying tribute to one of their own in the house he so loved.

Words flowed just as elegantly from the night's speakers, including legendary songwriter Kristofferson, who recounted Johnny and June's love story; daughter Rosanne, who spoke of her father's lessons in "love, pain, and rhythm"; and Cash's longtime bass player Marshall Grant, who told a spellbound crowd how Cash's first band, The Tennessee Two, came together and stumbled upon the signature rhythm that defined Cash's sound. Former Vice President Al Gore read aloud the lyrics to "The Man in Black," Cash's anthem for the downtrodden. Once again, the Ryman proved its capacity for channeling reverence, dignity, and heartfelt emotion. These were the attributes that Cash knew well and the reason why his memorial could not have been held anywhere else.

The Ryman has remained a remarkably solid and steadfast presence in Nashville's skyline since 1892, surviving destructive tornadoes that blew through downtown in 1897, 1933, and 1998, more than a few fire scares, and major flooding in 1927, 1975, and 2010. The structure itself has required only routine maintenance, with only the mechanical and electrical systems requiring periodic upgrades. By 2012, the Ryman stage, which had been in place since 1951, was showing wear and tear that routine maintenance could not remedy. It became evident that replacing the stage was necessary. On February 3, 2012, a special Grand Ole Opry featuring Keith Urban, Charley Pride, and The Oak Ridge Boys was the last event held on the well-worn 1951 stage. Seventeen days of delicate construction under watchful eyes later, The Band Perry made their sold-out Ryman headlining debut. "To play the Ryman is to step into country music's rich history and we are honored to perform there…we promise to inaugurate the new stage with all the respect and reverence it deserves," said Kimberly, Reid, and Neil Perry.

In addition to an improved performance surface, the newly reinforced stage provides triple the load-bearing capacity to ensure it will safely withstand the strenuous production requirements of modern events. To honor six decades of performances on the old stage, and to give performers and tourists alike the opportunity to stand where so many greats appeared, the front three feet of the new stage is laid with planks salvaged from the legendary 1951 stage.

As the world progressed headlong into the information age at the turn of the century, buzz about the Ryman's rich entertainment history and unparalleled acoustics reached artists and fans of every genre around the globe. It became a must-play destination for artists on the rise and landed on the "bucket list" of many renowned veterans. For superstars like James Taylor, Neil Young, Paul Simon, and Van Morrison, performing at the Ryman is a career milestone important enough that they have forgone opportunities to play much larger venues, choosing to play the Ryman instead. Top-selling contemporary artists across the genres have shown the same reverence. Alison Krauss, Dave Chappelle, Eddie Vedder, Kings

John Legend serenades a full house at the Ryman during his 2006 concert.

Brian Wagner photograph, Ryman Auditorium Archives

of Leon, Keith Urban, Mumford & Sons, and Widespread Panic are among the artists who have played multiple consecutive nights in order to create the kind of intimate concert experience that could not happen in a larger venue.

The sense of connection between performers and the audience that the Ryman is known to create can be attributed to more than just the relatively small size of the room. The auditorium's oak pews curve to embrace the stage, placing the audience close to the performers and, with no divisions between seats, close to each other. The arrangement allows artists to look the audience in the eyes, hear everything in the room, and feel the energy of the crowd. This unique Ryman experience, which leads fans and performers alike to rank the venue as their favorite, has not been lost on the media or the music industry. Both have praised the theatre with accolades and awards.

Rolling Stone magazine dubbed the Ryman "God's listening room," and their readers ranked the hall as one of the best venues in America. The Ryman has been named "Theatre of the Year" by *Pollstar Magazine*, the ACM's "Venue of the Year," the "SRO Venue of the Year," presented by the CMA, and the IEBA's "Venue of the Year" on multiple occasions. Leading tourism website Trip Advisor awarded their "Certificate of Excellence" to the Ryman. This special award is only given to businesses that rank in the top ten percent worldwide for traveler feedback.

But perhaps the greatest testimonials to the joy of playing the Ryman are from the artists, who rarely fail to acknowledge from the stage how thrilling it is to be there. Keith Urban called performing at the Ryman "the coolest gig in the universe...perhaps beyond!" Neil Young likened playing the venue to "coming home." Another artist to sing its praises was Chris Martin, lead singer of the English pop group Coldplay, when he called the Ryman "The greatest venue in the world!" "This is possibly the coolest place we've ever played," he said during the critically acclaimed concert. "It's the first time in about nine years that I've thought we sounded tremendously good. So many of our heroes have played here, from Johnny Cash all the way through to Johnny Cash, including Johnny Cash." While on a tour stop in Boston, famed rocker Roger Daltrey agreed with Martin's assessment and spoke even more plainly: "That's the best bloody place for a musician to play in the whole...world!"

Being situated at the epicenter of Music City, home to more musicians than any other place on the planet, the Ryman shows often treat audiences to collaborations that would not happen anywhere else. Regular performers Old Crow Medicine Show have not only sold out many of their own concerts at the Ryman, but have appeared as surprise guests at performances by friends such as Dierks Bentley, Mumford & Sons, and Emmylou Harris. From Jack White popping in for a few songs with Bob Dylan, to Barry Gibb delighting the audience at a Ricky Skaggs concert, to Steve Cropper with Peter Frampton, Taylor Swift with the Civil Wars, and Vince Gill with just about everyone, the surprises never fail to create one-of-a kind musical memories. The parade of guests was so powerful when

Levon Helm brought his *Ramble* to the Ryman for the first time in 2007, the decision was made to repeat and record the show in 2011, resulting in a Grammy-winning live album and a concert film that aired nationwide on public television.

In addition to inviting guest performers, many artists break away from their standard set lists to include classic country songs in honor of the stage they stand upon. Others step away from the microphones for a spine-tingling a cappella performance that allows the singers and their audiences to experience the amazing acoustics for which the room will forever be revered. As Ketch Secor of Old Crow Medicine show said, "It's not when you go to Nashville you got to play the Ryman. It's when you play in *America*, you've got to play the Ryman Auditorium. It's that kind of a touchstone for all of the artists who stand on that stage."

Nashville has long prided itself on being a progressive city—and not just a Southern city or an American city—but a city of the world. Since its doors opened in 1892, Ryman Auditorium has contributed mightily to that cause, welcoming world-class entertainment, leading educators, reformers, and politicians, and visitors from across the globe. For all who have had the singular experience of performing on the historic stage, enjoying the magic of a Ryman concert, or wandering through the national historic landmark and soaking in its stories—and for all who hope to—it is important to remember the efforts of those who inspired, built, supported, and preserved the hall for our enjoyment today.

From divine inspiration to single-minded determination, Thomas G. Ryman worked tirelessly to raise funds and build a place where all could worship. Lula C. Naff, the legendary female impresario who brought a staggering array of the world's finest talent to the stage, used her grit and business acumen to cultivate a love for the arts among Nashvillians, and in the process put the building and its tenuous future on solid financial footing. Perhaps no two individuals have played a larger role in the Ryman story.

Equally significant are the institutions that have defined essential parts of the Ryman's identity. The building will remain forever connected to its long-time tenant, the Grand Ole Opry, which drew millions of fans to experience country music's greatest show in person and introduced even more to the Ryman as the "Mother Church of Country Music" in their own living rooms via the 50,000 watt signal of WSM radio. As bluegrass was born and hillbilly music evolved into country music, thousands of hopefuls were drawn to the stage door in the back alley, seeking to join the boisterous, illustrious family that is the Grand Ole Opry—and some of them even made it.

Everyone knew it was the end of an era when the Grand Ole Opry left the building, but when the claim was made that the Ryman had finally outlived its usefulness, preservationists, country music fans, and concerned citizens rallied across the country, and in the end, the venerable old building was saved. Then, after a long period of benign neglect, when new owner Gaylord Entertainment made the commitment to restore Nashville's cultural heart, the Ryman roared back to life stronger than ever and is now appreciated on a level not possible without the perspective of time.

Thomas Ryman's vision for the Union Gospel Tabernacle was an ecumenical one. All souls were worthy of salvation regardless of race, denomination, or social status. As soon as the doors opened, Nashville's citizens claimed the auditorium as their own and quickly expanded on Ryman's original intention by booking entertainment, education, and civic events to fill the hall, bringing thousands together for communal experiences that were perhaps not exactly what Ryman imagined, but were experiences of vital importance to the city as they fostered fresh perspectives and a connection to the world at large. Ryman Auditorium became the place where Nashville met the world—and a wonderful place for the world to meet Nashville. Today, as people come together to enjoy a show, take a tour, or take the stage, the stories and the spirits of the people who have shepherded the beloved building are undeniably present, making the special moments all the richer. And, in these moments, the spark of Tom Ryman's dream still burns bright.

Selected Sources & Bibliography

Adams, George Rollie and Ralph Jerry Christian. Nashville: A Political History. Rev. ed. Virginia Beach, Virginia: Donning Company, 1988.

Axthelm, Pete. "A Tribute to the Ryman from the Bar at Tootsie's." Newsweek. 25 March 1974, 69.

Betts, Ann. "The Best One Night Stand in the Country." Premiere. 5, no. 3 (Spring/Summer 1985): 10-15.

Brumbaugh, Thomas B., Martha I. Strayhorn, and Gary G. Gore, eds., Architecture of Middle Tennessee: The Historic American Buildings Survey. Chicago, Illinois: University of Illinois Press, 1974, 40-47.

Cash, Johnny. Man in Black. Grand Rapids, Michigan: Zondervan Publishing House, 1975.

Charles S. Mitchell Collection. Vanderbilt University Library Special Collections. Donated by Jesse Wills.

Coke, Fletch. Captain Ryman at Home: His Family and Neighbors on Rutledge Hill. Nashville, Tennessee: J&J Printers, 1982.

Cornell, Elizabeth. "New Life for the Capitol of Country," Historic Preservation News. June/July 1994, 8ff.

Cunniff, Albert. "Muscle Behind the Music: The Life and Times of Jim Denny." Journal of Country Music. 11, no. 1 (1986). Part I: "The Path to Power."

Custer, Jack E. "Captain Tom Ryman: The Man, the Myth, the Paradox." Waterways Journal. 27 Jan. 1979, 11-81.

_____. "Capt. Ryman Revisited (or) Filling in the Gaps." Waterways Journal. 8 Feb. 1980, 5-31.

Daily American. (Dates indicated in text.)

Danker, Frederick E. "Country Music and the Mass Media: The Johnny Cash Television Show." Popular Music and Society. 2, no. 2 (Winter 1973): 124-44.

Darden Family Papers. Tennessee State Library and Archives (V-B-5, Ac-657).

Davis, Louise. "Steamboatin' Tom Ryman and His Gift to Nashville." Tennessean Magazine. 27 Jan. 1974, 4-9.

_____. "When Captain Tom 'Got Religion.'" Tennessean Magazine. 3 Feb. 1974, 12-16.

_____. "The Men Who Built the Ryman." Tennessean Magazine. 10 March 1974, 8-13.

Davidson, Bill. "Thar's Gold in Them Thar Hillbilly Tunes." Colliers. 28 July 1954, 34ff.

Donelson, Bettie M. Papers. Tennessee State Library and Archives (II-E-2-3, 309).

Douglas, Byrd. Steamboatin' on the Cumberland. Nashville, Tennessee: Tennessee Book Company, 1961.

Doyle, Don H. Nashville in the New South, 1880-1930. Knoxville, Tennessee: University of Tennessee Press, 1985.

_____. Nashville Since the 1920s. Knoxville, Tennessee: University of Tennessee Press, 1985.

Ewing, David. "Ewing: Higher Ground." Nashville City Paper. 14 June 2010.

Flamming, James Douglas. "The Sam Jones Revivals and Social Reform in Nashville, Tennessee, 1885-1900." (M.A. Thesis, Vanderbilt University) Nashville, Tennessee, 1983.

Francis Robinson Papers. Vanderbilt University Library Special Collections.

Gaylord Entertainment Company. The Ryman Remembers: Recipes & Recollections. Nashville, Tennessee: Gaylord Entertainment Company, 1996.

Gossett, Charmaine B., ed. Captain Tom Ryman: His Life and Legacy. Franklin, Tennessee: Hillsboro Press, 2001.

Graham, Eleanor, ed. Nashville: A Short History and Selected Buildings. Nashville, Tennessee: Historical Commission of Metro-Nashville-Davidson County, 1974.

Grand Ole Opry Collection. Vanderbilt University Library Special Collections.

Hagan, Chet. Grand Ole Opry: The Official History. New York: Henry Holt & Co., 1989.

_____. Country Music Legends in the Hall of Fame. Nashville, Tennessee: Thomas Nelson Publishers, 1982.

Havighurst, Craig. Air Castle of the South: WSM and the Making of Music City. Champaign, Illinois: University of Illinois Press, 2007.

Hemphill, Paul. The Nashville Sound: Bright Lights and Country Music. New York: Simon & Schuster, 1970.

Henderson, Jerry. "A History of the Ryman Auditorium in Nashville, Tennessee, 1892-1920." (Doctoral Dissertation, Louisiana State University) Baton Rouge, Louisiana, 1962.

_____. "Nashville's Ryman Auditorium." Tennessee Historical Quarterly. 27 (Winter, 1968): 302-28.

_____. "The Ryman Auditorium, Its Years as a Religious Center of Nashville and the South." (Unpublished paper) Tennessee State Library and Archives, W-E-1, Box 1, f. 9.

Holcomb, Walt. Sam Jones: An Ambassador of the Almighty. Nashville, Tennessee: Methodist Publishing, 1947.

Hope, Bob. "It Says Here." King Features Syndicate Press Release. Jan. 27, 1949.

Incorporation Documents. Official Records Book of Davidson County. Copies made available with corporate books, letters, and files of the Auditorium Improvement Company in possession of Mr. Roy A. Miles, Jr., Nashville, Tennessee.

Jones, Laura McElwain. The Life and Sayings of Sam P. Jones. Atlanta, Georgia: J.L. Nichols, 1907.

Jones, Sam P. Papers. Special Collections, Robert W. Woodruff Library, Emory University, Atlanta, Georgia.

_____. Papers. Hargrett Rare Book and Manuscript Library, University of Georgia Libraries, Athens, Georgia.

_____. Thunderbolts: Comprising Most Elegant Reasonings, Delightful Narratives, Poetic and Pathetic Incidents, Caustic and Unmerciful Flagellation of Sin, Together with Irresistible Appeal to the Higher Sensibilities of Man to Quit His Meanness and Do Right. Nashville, Tennessee: Sam P. Jones, 1896.

Jeter Smith Dance Collection. Nashville Room, Nashville Davidson County Public Library.

Keillor, Garrison. "Onward and Upward with the Arts at the Opry." New Yorker. 6 May 1974, 46-48.

Kreyling, Christine. "Hallowed Hall: Saving The Ryman, We Saved Our Own Soul." The Nashville Scene. Sept. 8, 1994.

Malone, Bill C. Country Music USA. Austin, Texas: University of Texas Press, 1968.

McLoughlin, Jr., William G. Modern Revivalism: Charles Grandison Finney to Billy Graham. New York: Ronald Press, 1959.

Miles, Jr., Roy A. "Obituary for a Grand Lady—The Ryman Auditorium." Speech, Vanderbilt University, 7 May 1973.

Moore, Scott. "A Country Music Shrine Opens Its Arms." The Washington Post. June 19, 1994.

Moore, Thurston, ed. Country Music Who's Who. Nashville, Tennessee: Heather Publications, 1966. See esp. p. 28 for Harry Stone, "Looking Back."

The Naff Collection. Nashville Room, Nashville-Davidson County Public Library.

Nashville Banner. (Dates indicated in text.)

Nashville Good News Weekly. (Dates indicated in text.)

Nashville This Week. (Dates indicated in text.)

Opry Picture/History Book. The Opry Observer. Nashville's Grand Ole Opry (text by Jack Hurst). All published in several editions by the Grand Ole Opry, Nashville, Tennessee.

Pemberton, Brock. "The Theatre's 'Road' Staging a Comeback, but it is a Much Changed Road," New York Times Magazine. 20 Aug. 1939, copy s.p.

Pope, Bill. "Fiery Sam Jones Rose to Leading Evangelist." Atlanta Constitution. 21 Nov. 1961, 6.

Pugh, Ronnie. "Ernest Tubb's Performing Career: Broadcast, Stage and Screen." Journal of Country Music. 7, no. 3 (Dec. 1978): 67-83.

Rensi, Raymond Charles. "Sam Jones: Southern Evangelist." (Doctoral Dissertation, University of Georgia) Athens, Georgia, 1971.

Rivers, Jerry. Hank Williams, From Life to Legend. 2nd ed. Nashville, Tennessee: Jerry Rivers, 1980

Rumble, John. "The Emergence of Nashville as a Recording Center: Logbooks from the Castle Studio, 1952-53." Journal of Country Music. 7, no. 3 (Dec. 1978): 22-41.

Ryman Family Papers, 1841-1973. Tennessee State Library and Archives (V-L-5, Ac 81-15).

Schlappi, Elizabeth. Roy Acuff: The Smoky Mountain Boy. Gretna, Louisiana: Pelican Publishing, 1978.

Smith, John L., compiler. The Johnny Cash Discography. Westport, Connecticut: Greenwood Press, 1985.

The Nashville Review. (Dates indicated in text.)

The Tennessean. (Dates indicated in text.)

Thomas, Sr., Jack. The Nashville I Knew. Nashville, Tennessee: Thomas Nelson Publishers, 1984.

Wilhelmina Webb Collection. Metropolitan Nashville-Davidson County Archives.

Wilson, Richard L. "Sam Jones: An Apostle of the New South." Georgia Historical Quarterly. 57 (1983).

WSM Radio/Television Collection. Vanderbilt University Library Special Collections. Donated by Jesse Wills.